HOW CHILDREN CONSTRUCT LITERACY

**Piagetian
Perspectives**

Yetta M. Goodman
University of Arizona

Editor

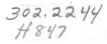
International Reading Association
800 Barksdale Road, PO Box 8139
Newark, Delaware 19714-8139

The International Reading Association attempts, through its publications, to provide a forum for a wide spectrum of opinions on reading. This policy permits divergent viewpoints without assuming the endorsement of the Association.

I would like to thank the outstanding graduate students who were involved in the evolution of this volume.

YMG

Cover design by Boni Nash
Cover photo by Laima Druskis
Photos in Chapter 6 provided by Esther Pillar Grossi

Contents

5

6

7

Foreword

O ne part of the endless source of interest in Piaget is the seemingly inexhaustible depth of his theory. Another is the kind of
conversation he developed as a way of finding out what children
think about things. We owe him both a methodology and an absolutely fascinating set of improbable questions: Does a mountain
really change shape as you drive around it? Where are dreams?
What happens to the weight of a chunk of clay when you break it
into little pieces? Is water in a tilted bottle also tilted? Is a road as
long when you walk down it as when you walk up?

The groundbreaking work of Ferreiro follows in this tradition. She has found similarly improbable questions to ask about
reading and writing. For instance, in the sentence, "Mama baked
three cakes," young children may believe that one of the words represents Mama and the other three represent the three cakes. This
fact strikes me as an insight as surprising and as powerful as Piaget's
discoveries about the conservation of number.

Such an insight is not simple curiosity. One of Piaget's most
significant contributions to education is helping us realize that the
headway children make when they are constructing their own sense
sometimes looks like a move backwards. Ideas that worked in certain circumstances are combined with other ideas in a search for
something that works universally. But the new combination takes
awhile to build. And, in the meantime, while the ideas are in the
process of being combined, they do not work nearly as well. If we
do not know what to look for, we might well believe that the children
are regressing.

Piaget, in general, and Ferreiro, in this book, give us indicators we never would have recognized otherwise. Grossi provides a fine example in Chapter 6. Some of the children came to school having memorized how to write their names. But they had not yet realized that there is a connection between writing and pronunciation. As they came to construct this understanding, they started applying it to the writing of their own names. Esther, for example, who had been writing her name correctly, started writing ET, consistent with her new understanding that each letter represents some sound — in her view so far, a syllable. This is not yet a wholly adequate understanding, but it is an important step in the right direction, even though for the time being it conflicts with the correct writing of her name.

Such "rich conflict[s]," to use Grossi's terms, enlist children's own powerful intelligence in the construction of their understanding. The studies in this book should contribute toward providing such experiences for young children who are learning about reading and writing.

Eleanor Duckworth
Harvard University

Contributors

Emilia Ferreiro
Center of Research
and Advanced Studies
National Polytechnic Institute
Mexico

Yetta M. Goodman
Division of Language,
Reading, and Culture
University of Arizona
Tucson, Arizona, USA

Esther Pillar Grossi
GEEMPA
Porto Alegre, Brazil

Clotilde Pontecorvo
University of Rome
Rome, Italy

Ana Teberosky
Municipal Institute of Education
Barcelona, Spain

Liliana Tolchinsky Landsmann
University of Tel Aviv
Tel Aviv, Israel

Cristina Zucchermaglio
Rome, Italy

Yetta M. Goodman

Discovering Children's Inventions of Written Language

"To understand children we must hear their words, follow their explanations, understand their frustrations, and listen to their logic" (Ferreiro & Teberosky, 1982).

Discovering the knowledge children have about reading and writing systems has, for a long time, excited researchers interested in language. Teachers and other researchers observed children as they read books and used pencils and crayons to express their meanings. Their observations allowed them to speculate that children even before the age of 5 knew a great deal about written language.

As early as 1898, Harriet Iredell, a Pennsylvania teacher, wrote an article about her study of common reading and writing experiences that children were immersed in before they came to school.

Three-year-old Harold takes a book to his father. "Read a story," he begs. The father lifts him to his knee and reads, the book open before them both. There are occasional interruptions when both look at the pictures illustrating the text. Or he brings the book and says: "I read a story," and turning the pages, following the text with his eyes, he improvises as he goes, a tale which is a compound of what he has heard and his own imaginings. Harold is learning to read.

A letter has been received, read and discussed by several members of the family. It is then laid on the table, Harold takes it up. He looks it over and walks around thoughtfully with it under his arm. Presently, turning up the blank side of the sheet, he says, "I want to write." He is supplied with paper and pencil, and seated in his little chair, is much occupied for five minutes. He then takes the scrawled-over sheet to his grandmother, with the request that she read it. Does she hesitate? Not at all. She promptly reads from it such sentences as he might have given expression to, greatly to his joy and satisfaction. He is learning to write (p. 235).

In the 1920s, Vygotsky, a Soviet psychologist, raised questions about the degree of authenticity that was embedded in the kinds of writing Montessori was assigning her students in Italy. Vygotsky argued: "...the basic contradiction that appears in the teaching of writing not only in Montessori's school but in most other schools...[is] that writing is taught as a motor skill and not as a complex cultural activity....writing must be 'relevant to life'..." (1978, pp. 117, 118). Both of these early twentieth century psychologists were aware of the ability young children had to participate in writing experiences. Some of the arguments pursued today concerning teaching young children to read and write can be seen in their writings.

During the child study movement of the 1920s and 1930s, Gesell and Ilg (1946) documented children's book handling and writing behaviors in the United States. In the 1930s, researchers such as Hildreth (1936) in the United States and Legrun (1932) in Germany studied the writing development of preschool children not yet involved in schooling experiences and were able to categorize and describe the orthography and strategies the children were using in a systematic fashion.

However, it wasn't until the 1970s that researchers began to study in great depth the variety of explicit and intuitive concepts children had about the nature of reading and writing systems and to document what functions young children thought reading and writing served in their lives.

It is interesting to speculate why it took so long to see the development of writing in young children. There has been continued interest in the development of children's artwork (Gardner, 1980; Kellogg, 1969). Although there is mention in passing of the writing embedded in the artistic scribbles of children, generally these researchers seemed to overlook the significance of the evidence of children's writing contained within children's art. This is a good example of researchers totally missing data because they aren't looking for it. Since early scribbles were not yet being identified as writing, researchers were not paying much attention to their significance. The evidence was there, but researchers weren't expecting to discover that children were inventing written language. Ferreiro states later in this book that "we see what we know."

Other educators and researchers preoccupied with how to teach kids to read and write ignored that children were already learning to read and write as they were reading and writing to learn. Heath (1983) shares this insight in her exploration of children's writing and reading before they go to school.

As a number of scholars began to suspect that kids came to school with knowledge about literacy and began to disseminate their hypotheses and conclusions to others, the field of studying the literacy learning of preschool children began to develop and build on the work of earlier scholars. We began to share in books and at conferences the exciting discoveries that people were making about young children (Goodman, Haussler, & Strickland, 1981; Jaggar & Smith-Burke, 1985; Pinnell & Matlin, 1989).

Many researchers, coming from different fields of study with different orientations, were asking questions about how children come to know written language. Some were finding their answers through naturalistic research, gathering information and observations in the real life settings of children's home and school experiences, while others were collecting data through experimental studies.

A group of educationists wanted to know what children knew about literacy before they came to school and how they came to know it. They studied children's responses to print in the home and school environment and concluded that children knew a good deal about writing, especially as it reflected their experiences with print (Bissex, 1980; Goodman & Altwerger, 1981; Harste, Woodward, & Burke, 1984; Teale & Sulzby, 1986).

Anthropologists and social historians wondered what influences the society, the community, the family, and the social nature of the classroom had on literacy development and have provided important accounts about such influences, especially relating to social class differences (Anderson & Stokes, 1984; Heath, 1983; Scollon & Scollon, 1984; Shieffelin & Cochran-Smith, 1984).

Psychologists wondered how children came to understand what literacy is, what functions children believed literacy served in their own lives, and how children made use of literacy (Clark, 1976; Clay, 1975; Downing, 1971; Wells, 1986). Linguists wondered what knowledge children had about the various linguistic systems such as phonology, orthography, syntax, and semantics. They began to explore what children knew about written language and how this differed from their knowledge of oral language (Cazden, 1972; Clay, 1975; Read, 1975). Through ethnographies and formal observational studies, various researchers interpreted what children's interactions with written language meant and what influence these interactions had on their development of writing and reading (Dyson, 1982; Harste, Woodward, & Burke, 1984; Taylor, 1983; Taylor & Dorsey-Gaines, 1988; Teale & Sulzby, 1986). Others used experimental designs to add to the data about early literacy development (Ehri, 1975, 1976; Mason, 1980).

The research on early literacy has come from a broad group of researchers with different beliefs about knowledge and truth, the relationships between teaching and learning, language and language learning, and the purposes and methodologies of research itself. This very diversity allows groups of like-minded researchers or individuals to use the knowledge being generated by others to expand on their own developing theories of literacy development.

Psychogenesis and Literacy Development

Scientists ask questions and find ways to answer them based on their own views of truth and within the traditions they have evolved (Erickson, 1986). Researchers ask questions and organize their research in keeping with their beliefs about what constitutes knowledge and data. It is not surprising, therefore, that when a group of Piagetian psychologists began to ask questions about what young children know about written language, they would embark on their search using the clinical approach developed by Jean Piaget. Led by the insights of Emilia Ferreiro, a group of Piagetian psychologists began asking questions similar to those being asked by other literacy development researchers. Both their questions and method of seeking answers reflected their different orientation and beliefs about the nature of knowledge, language, and child development.

Piaget's (1976) work has had immense impact on the understanding of how children come to know their world. The important contributions that his clinical approach made to the understanding of the world of childhood cannot be underestimated. Even his critics build on his understandings, his concepts, and his methodology (Vygotsky, 1987).

Humans have a history. Their history represents not only what they have experienced day by day throughout their own lives, but also encompasses their inclusion in a family, a community, and a culture. Participation in the mundane literacy events—daily immersion with reading and writing experiences—of the family, the community, and the various subcultures in which humans constantly and continuously coexist is also part of the human history.

Piagetians, especially, help those working with children understand how important it is to recognize the significance of such a history on the development of the knowledge of each individual. By observing children's interactions with literacy events, Ferreiro and her colleagues in Argentina began to raise questions about the understandings children develop over time concerning reading and writing. Based on their scientific knowledge of language and learning and the questions they were raising, these Piagetian psychologists developed a set of literacy tasks with which children could interact.

These tasks were stimulated by a series of questions they were asking about literacy learning.

- How do children decide what is readable?

- How do they compose written language?
- How do they become aware of the forms written language takes?
- How do children understand and differentiate the roles that drawing, illustrations, numbers, cursive writing, and print play in the writing system?
- How do children see the object known as writing as different from the object known as drawing?
- What units of language do children expect to find in the written text?
- In what contexts do children expect to find different genres such as fiction, news stories, or oral conversations?
- What knowledge do children hold about written language, and how do children's perceptions of their knowledge change over time?

Answers to many of these questions already have been published elsewhere (Ferreiro, 1978, 1984, 1985, 1986; Ferreiro & Teberosky, 1979, 1982), and some are addressed in this book. Furthermore, new questions are continuously emerging. Scholars are especially interested in discovering the hypotheses children make about written language that are original constructions. Scholars call these original hypotheses *psychogenetic development*. For our purposes in this volume, *psychogenesis* can be defined as the history of an idea or concept as influenced by the learner's personal intellectual activity. Psychogenetic development can be compared with *sociogenetic development*—those hypotheses attributed to cultural transmissions on the part of adults. It is because of their questions about the knowledge that children develop in response to the objects of the culture that the careful, in-depth observations of the Piagetian researchers often reveal levels of development that occur at particular moments in a child's history.

Ferreiro, Teberosky, and their colleagues gave children newspapers and books to read and asked children to write names of people and other familiar animate and inanimate objects. They also asked children to read and write isolated words, sentences, and various orthographic features based on their understandings of linguistics and always to consider the relationship of these units to larger texts. Through their inquiries, the researchers gained understanding of how children come to know the written language system—its form, its uses and purposes, and its relationship to the objects within the culture.

An important aspect of the clinical approach includes explicating children's thinking by asking them to explain why they give particular responses and especially to explain their contradictions. In this way, the researchers see the degree to which children are consistent about their understandings and gain insights into why the children come to the concepts they hold about writing and reading at a particular time in their life's history.

The researchers do not tell the children that they are wrong or inconsistent but leave the children's contradictions unresolved, believing that through future interactions with the same or similar objects and daily experiences with written language, the children will adapt their conceptualizations. The contradictions children hold reveal important information about their developing conceptualizations. Through their questioning, Piagetian researchers come to understand the particular concepts that the children are holding, which ones they are willing to give up, and when they are willing to move to new understandings about the written language system they are discovering.

Early Piagetian literacy studies have been conducted in Spanish in Argentina and Mexico City, in French in Geneva, Switzerland, and with bilingual children in Spain (Ferreiro & Teberosky, 1982b). These studies and related ones have been extended to different countries, different languages, and different social settings. The articles in this book represent some of these extensions.

Tolchinsky Landsmann, working in Israel, adds the dimension of Israeli children working with the Hebrew alphabetic system. Teberosky and Pontecorvo and Zucchermaglio extend the research by answering similar questions about literacy development using clinical methodology in classroom settings where children show the influences of peers and teachers on their conceptualizations of reading and writing. Using Piagetian methodology in classroom settings moves issues concerning literacy learning into a social context and makes the results of the research especially relevant to educational institutions.

By studying not only the role of the learner but also the influences of teachers in the development of literacy, these Piagetian researchers demonstrate the significance of teachers' questioning strategies in moving children toward an examination of their contradictions. The collaboration among peers as they work on the same kind of literacy task provides insight into how young children influence one another's learning as they encourage one another to think about language in new and different ways.

Studying literacy development in classrooms also has resulted in dynamic changes in the relationship between the researcher and the teacher, as shown by Pontecorvo and Zucchermaglio and Grossi (this volume). Teachers become part of the research team and eventually better understand their role as decisionmakers in the classroom, becoming more informed by their own inquiries into the nature of literacy. They become confident in asking their own questions about the nature of literacy and literacy learning.

An Overview of the Chapters

The chapters that follow were originally presented as papers at the International Reading Association's Eleventh World Congress on Reading, held in London in 1986. Emilia Ferreiro encouraged the presenters at that time to consider three major questions that became the organizing focus for the presentations and the written papers, which became the manuscript for this book:

1. What evidence is there of a line of literacy development among the children you are working with now that is similar to the concepts that emerged from the research with the Argentinean children?

2. What are the general principles that guide your research in the field of education?

3. How do you perceive the relationship between psychological theory and educational practice?

Each of the researchers has addressed these questions, and a synopsis of each of the chapters with information about the authors' professional affiliations follows.

Emilia Ferreiro is at the Center for Research and Advanced Studies at the National Polytechnic Institute of Mexico. She received her doctorate in Geneva with Jean Piaget. The idea of psychogenesis of literacy development basically has stemmed from her innovative procedures and continuous research with children in Argentina, Mexico, and Switzerland. The Argentinean study by Ferreiro and Teberosky has been translated from Spanish (1979) into Italian and Portuguese and is available in English as *Literacy before Schooling* (1982).

In her chapter, Ferreiro sketches the results of more than a decade of research on the evolution of literacy development. She presents basic points about the theoretical framework that informs her work and the work of those involved in literacy development research using clinical approach procedures. She concludes with the implications her research has for teachers, researchers, diagnosticians, curriculum developers, and other related professionals.

Liliana Tolchinsky Landsmann is a psychologist at Tel Aviv University in the School of Education and Department of Occupational Therapy, where she is involved in teaching courses on cognitive development and written language development. She is an educational advisor to the Israeli Television Center. She has collaborated with Ferreiro and Teberosky for many years and was part of the research team in Argentina. When she moved to Israel in 1976, she continued to follow a similar line of research in Hebrew in collaboration with Iris Levin.

In her chapter, Tolchinsky Landsmann takes the evolution of writing as described by Ferreiro and examines it within the constraints of the Hebrew language as produced by Israeli children. She raises questions about literacy development as it is influenced by a very different writing system from the one used in earlier psychogenetic literacy research. Using this different system provides insight into the constraints that the written language system itself has on literacy development. Tolchinsky Landsmann also suggests implications and applications of her work for educational practice.

Ana Teberosky, an educational psychologist, is concerned with the applications from psychogenetic literacy research to literacy education and continues her research within the classroom setting in order to combine research and instructional practices. She has been working at the Municipal Institute of Education in Barcelona for 12 years, focusing on what impact the collaboration of children in bilingual settings has on their literacy development. Prior to her appointment in Spain, she was at a Buenos Aires university in Argentina, where she worked with Ferreiro. She is coauthor with Ferreiro of *Literacy before Schooling* (1982).

Teberosky's chapter presents her latest work with Catalan and Spanish bilingual children interacting with their peers and teachers in order to write captions for different kinds of pictures. She categorizes the children's responses, using syntactic analysis to show their sensitivity in providing a variety of responses depending upon the nature of the pictures being used. She highlights the influences of contextual differences on the development of literacy.

Clotilde Pontecorvo is a professor of educational psychology at the University of Rome, where she is the director of the Developmental Psychology Department. Her work has focused on understanding how cognitive processes develop through curriculum, especially in the fields of various natural and social science disciplines. One of her main concerns is discourse processes as they develop through discussion and argumentation among children in school settings. She uses approaches from both Piagetian and Vygotskian research to inquire into the knowledge children develop.

Her coauthor, Cristina Zucchermaglio, was Clotilde Pontecorvo's doctoral student at the time this paper was originally written. She is now director of management training at a national software company. At the same time, she continues to collaborate with the staff at the Center for the Study of Literacy Development at the University of Rome concerning issues of language and the computer. Her book on literacy development is soon to be published.

Pontecorvo and Zucchermaglio's chapter explores the role of the social context of the classroom in fostering the development of literacy in children through interaction with teachers and peers. The authors categorize different types of social interactions that are involved in the literacy learning of young children and how these interactions impact their abilities to work productively and cooperatively with others. The power of the influence of the social context of the classroom becomes evident.

Esther Pillar Grossi is now the Secretary of Education for Porto Alegre, Brazil. She has a doctorate in cognitive psychology from Paris, although her original studies were in the field of mathematics. She has been a member of the study group known as GEEMPA (Groupo de Estudo Sobre Educacao-Metodologia de Pesquisa e Acao), which is supported by the Brazilian government and an American foundation concerned with action research in educational methodology in Porto Alegre in South Brazil. In her role as an educational consultant, she was responsible for introducing to two provinces in Brazil a view of literacy development using theory and knowledge from psychogenetic literacy development research.

Grossi's chapter presents the experiences of the GEEMPA group as it applied the knowledge from the psychogenesis of literacy development to a complex educational setting. She explains how the classroom is organized to capitalize on literacy events of various kinds. She indicates how the classroom experience can inform ongoing research in order to make appropriate adaptations for specific settings.

The work on psychogenesis and literacy development has had great influence on the development of my ideas and my research agenda in relation to how children learn to read and write. I have been fortunate to participate and interact with this group of researchers over the years and to learn from them as well as from the children with whom I have been working. My experiences with this team have increased my awareness of the symbiotic relationship between teaching and learning and have made me even more aware that the relationship can never be an isomorphic one. I express my gratitude to the authors of the chapters in this book for extending my own visions.

Literacy Development: Psychogenesis

T his chapter summarizes the major conclusions of several years of research on the evolution of literacy development. The work is basic research on the psychogenesis of the interpretation systems children build in order to understand the alphabetic representation of the language. The research was carried out mainly in Argentina and in Mexico on children with Spanish as their mother tongue, with the first results being published in 1979 (Ferreiro & Teberosky, 1979, 1982). I am still engaged in this kind of research.

The pedagogical implications of the results of the research were clear from the very beginning, and many colleagues in different countries—some of whom are authors in this volume—elaborated on these ideas and put them into pedagogical practice. An encouraging feature in these developments was the surprising fact that the differences in language did not constitute a barrier to the application of the basic ideas in a field so language dependent as literacy.

Perhaps the fact of having first studied the evolution of literacy development in Spanish, where the orthography is judged to be "simple" or, at least, with a letter/sound correspondence far more stable than in English, helped us look for the conceptual difficulties tied to the comprehension of a representational system. Spanish speaking children face specific difficulties in grasping the nature of the alphabetical writing system. These difficulties are not eliminated by the relative simplicity of the letter/sound correspondence, because they are prior to the alphabetical principles. That is the reason why similar and often identical difficulties are found in children speaking other languages and trying to learn other orthographies.

Basic Points of the Theoretical Framework

Before sketching the research results that provided the source of inspiration for the pedagogical experiences reported in subsequent chapters, I would like to clarify briefly some basic points of the general framework of the research I conducted with several collaborators and students.

1. We have studied *production* activities in children (i.e., writing), but our main interest is not writing as such. Similarly, we have studied *interpretation* activities in children (i.e., reading), but our main interest is not reading as such. In fact, the primary objective of our studies has been the understanding of the evolution of the systems of ideas children build up about the nature of the social object that is the writing system.

In order to know about the cognitive competence of children in this particular domain, we look into both their activities of production and their interpretation of written texts. We therefore studied children's performance, with the aim of making a theory about their competence, in keeping with a constructivist view of its evolution, rather than a theory about their performance. It is important to keep the competence/performance distinction in mind when we talk about the pedagogical implications of our empirical and theoretical findings.

2. Our findings support the general principles of Piaget's theory that receive specific interpretation in literacy development, such as the following:

- Children are not only learning subjects but also are knowing subjects. In other words, children acquire new behaviors during their development, but more importantly, they acquire new knowledge. This means that the writing system becomes an object of knowledge and can be characterized as such.

- In order to acquire knowledge about the writing system, children proceed the same way as in other domains of knowledge: They try to assimilate the information provided by the environment. But when the new information is impossible to assimilate, they very often are forced to reject it. They experiment with the object to find out about its properties, they experiment with the object to test their "hypothesis," they ask for information, and they try to make sense out of the mass of data they have assembled.

- It is precisely this last point—the search for coherence—that makes children build up interpretation systems in a developmentally ordered way. Such systems constitute something like "children's theories" about the nature and function of the writing system. As we repeatedly have tried to demonstrate, these children's theories are not a pale mirror image of what they have been told. The theories are real constructions that, more often than not, seem very strange to our adult way of thinking.

- These systems that children build during their development act as assimilation schemes, in Piaget's terms (1977). That is, these systems act as schemes through which information is interpreted, permitting children to make sense of their encounters with print and with print users. Once the systems are built, the schemes remain active (as any scheme does) without major changes, as long as they can fulfill the function of "making sense of the world."

- When new information repeatedly invalidates the scheme, children must engage in a difficult and sometimes painful process of modifying it. Usually, they first try to make small rearrangements to keep as much of the previous scheme as possible. However, at certain crucial points in the evolution, they feel compelled to reorganize their systems, keeping some of the preceding elements but redefining these elements as they become part of a new system. The need to incorporate new information is one of the reasons to change a given scheme. The other main reason to undertake such a hard task is the need to find internal consistency: for instance, when the results obtained from applying two different schemes lead to contradictory solutions.

Literacy Development as a Psychogenetic Process

For two reasons, I will briefly sketch the development of literacy competence in children by making reference to their written productions. The first reason is that written productions are easier to understand even when the audience does not have a precise knowledge of the mother tongue of the children. The second reason is that some of the written productions constitute a better way of having access to children's literacy competence. However, our way of looking into written productions is not limited to the written marks that children produce. We include the entire process of construction: the intentions, the comments and modifications introduced during the writing itself, and the interpretation that the "author" (the child) provides for his or her construction once it is finished.

We can distinguish three main developmentally ordered levels that I will summarize, each one with some subdivisions that I will not explain in detail (Ferreiro, 1986; Ferreiro & Teberosky, 1982).

First Level

At the beginning of the first level, children search for criteria in order to distinguish between the two basic modes of graphic representation: drawing and writing.

After a series of active explorations, children arrive at the following conclusion: The kinds of lines are not what allow us to distinguish between a drawing and a piece of writing. In fact, we produce both of them by using straight lines, curved lines, or dots. With the same kinds of lines, we can draw or write. The difference is in the way the lines are organized. When we draw, the lines are organized following the object's contours; when we write, the same lines do not follow the object's contours. When writing, we are outside the iconic domain. The letters' forms have nothing to do with the form of the object the letters are referring to, and their organization has nothing to do with the organization of the parts of the object.

With such a distinction, children very quickly recognize two of the basic characteristics of any writing system—that the set of forms is arbitrary (because letters do not reproduce the form of the objects), and that they are ordered in a linear fashion (whereas in drawing they are not). In fact, linearity and arbitrariness of forms are the two characteristics that appear very early in young children's written productions.

Although arbitrariness of forms does not necessarily imply conventionality, the conventional forms usually appear early in children's productions. Children do not apply their major efforts to inventing new letter forms; they accept the letter shapes from the society and very quickly adopt them. The children do not concentrate their efforts on the graphic elements as such but on the way these elements are organized (i.e., on the laws of the system).

Middle-class children who grow up in rich literacy environments usually recognize written marks as substitute objects during their third year of life. (The only function of substitute objects is to stand for other objects.) It was, however, by working with children from the slums, who do not have such a rich literacy environment, that we were able to identify the difficulties of the transition from "letters as objects" to "letters as substitute objects" (Ferreiro, 1984). Nevertheless, letters always can be treated as graphic objects. (They bear the generic name *letters*; they bear particular names; and they can be grouped in terms of their specific graphic characteristics.)

For our present purposes, it is enough to say that this first level in children's thinking produces two major accomplishments: (1) to consider strings of letters as substitute objects and (2) to make a clear distinction between two modes of graphic representation — the iconic mode (to draw) and the noniconic mode (to write).

These two acquisitions are permanent ones. Children subsequently will integrate them into more complex systems without giving them up.

Once the children have differentiated these two modes of graphic representation, a new problem arises. The children now need to discover the ways in which drawing and writing (which they previously have differentiated) relate to each other. The relationship between pictures and written text in a storybook, as well as similar relationships in environmental print or in their own graphic productions, poses a new problem for children that is solved with the following organizing principle: Letters are used to represent a property of the objects of the world (including human beings, animals, etc.) that drawing is unable to represent (i.e., their names).

Since letters represent the names of the objects, it is necessary for the children to begin to examine the ways letters are organized in order to represent the names adequately. The form of the objects represented is at the same time excluded, because children already know that written marks are placed outside the iconic domain. Therefore, children start looking for the conditions that a piece of writing ought to have in order to be a good representation of the object—to be "interpretable," "readable," or "good for saying something."

From this point on, children will face problems that are organized along two main directions—quantitative and qualitative. On the quantitative side, the first problem children face is the following: How many letters must a piece of writing have in order to be "readable"? This leads to the construction of one internal principle that we call the *principle of minimum quantity.*

Spanish speaking children (irrespective of their social or school background) choose three as the ideal number of letters. If there are three letters ordered, in a linear fashion, children are sure that "it must say something" ("ahi debe decir algo"). If there are only two letters, children are doubtful (some accept the possibility; others reject it). If there is only one letter, children are sure that they do not have something that can be read because, in their opinion, one letter is not enough to have a written word.

Three letters are enough. But this quantitative condition is not sufficient to have a good representation of a word, according to the children's conceptualizations. A qualitative condition also must be present: The letters must be different. If the piece of writing shows "the same letter all the time," children do not consider it to be a readable string. We call this second principle that regulates children's construction of knowledge *internal qualitative variations.* Freeman and Whitesell (1985) report data on English speaking children concerning the principles of minimum quantity and of internal quality variations.

Having these two organizing principles, children are able to look at each piece of writing and decide whether it is something that makes sense or whether it is only a string of letters that does not constitute a written representation of a word. Nevertheless, even with these two principles, children at this level still are unable to consider a set of written strings to discover which criteria are good ones to represent *differences in meaning.*

Second Level

A progressive control over the qualitative and quantitative variations leads to the construction of modes of differentiation between pieces of writing. This is one of the main accomplishments of the second developmental level. From this point on, children begin to look for objective differences in the written strings that justify different interpretations.

During the first level, children were satisfied with their own intentions. The strings could be objectively the same (from the point of view of an external observer), but if the child had the intention of writing a given noun in one of the strings and another noun in the other, they "said" different things in spite of graphic similarity. At this second level, the initial intentions are not enough. Now, children start to look for graphic differences that can support their different intentions. As they begin to maintain that two identical strings of letters cannot "say" different nouns, they consequently face a new problem: How can they create graphic differentiations making it possible to have different interpretations?

Again, children can work with the quantitative condition, with the qualitative one, or with both at the same time. For instance, the children notice that people sometimes write with few letters, sometimes with more letters. They wonder: What is the reason for these variations in the quantity of letters? These children are not analyzing the sound pattern of the word but are working with the linguistic symbol as a totality (meaning and sound together as a single entity).

As they search for the meaning and/or the referent of the noun they want to write, the children sometimes try to test the following hypothesis: Perhaps the variations in the number of letters are related to variations of quantifiable aspects of the referred objects (more letters if the referred object is big and fewer letters if it is small; more letters for a group of objects and fewer letters for a single object; more letters for an older person and fewer for a child).

Another possibility when looking for a reasonable way to control the quantitative variations is to establish a minimum and a maximum amount of letters for any written noun. The children may reason as follows: If a written representation must have at least three letters but no more than six or seven, then it is possible to create quantitative differentiations inside a given set of written productions. It is the context created by the other written words that determines the way to write a particular word.

Differentiation between pieces of writing also can be created, working on a qualitative direction. In this case, the following are possible solutions:

- If the child already possesses a large stock of graphic letter forms, he or she can use different letters for different words (without necessarily changing the quantity of letters).

- If the child has a limited stock of graphic letter forms, he or she can change only one or two letters (for instance, the first or the last one) to write a different word, with all the others remaining constant.

- Having a limited stock of graphic letter forms, the child also can obtain different representations by changing the position of the same letters in the linear order. This latter solution is the most striking one that children come to at this level of development.

Children also may try to control quantitative and qualitative variations at the same time. This implies an effort of coordination that is not easy.

It is important to keep in mind that the previously constructed principles remain unchanged: Minimum quantity and internal qualitative variations continue to regulate the construction of a written representation. These two principles do not suffice, however, to make comparisons between differently written nouns. What has been added now is the construction of a system of variations that integrates the previous principles but allows for a kind of *interrelational* comparison, the previous ones being *intrarelational* only (Ferreiro, 1986). It must be emphasized that all these efforts by the children to create ways of graphic differentiation in order to represent different words precedes any knowledge of the relationship between the sound pattern of the word and the written representation.

Third Level

The third level corresponds to the "phonetization" of the written representation. Spanish speaking children construct three well differentiated hypotheses during the period that characterizes this level: syllabic, syllabic-alphabetic, and alphabetic.

The access to the phonetization level is prepared by a lot of information children may receive from the environment. One of the most important pieces of written information is a child's own name. Children can accept that given strings of letters are necessary to "say" their names, but at a given point, they begin to look for some "intrinsic" rationality: Why precisely those letters and not others? Why that number of letters and not another? The resistance of the object in literacy development plays a similar role as the resistance of the object in other domains of knowledge (the object being, in this case, the written strings that are produced by adults).

The syllabic hypothesis is well documented in Spanish speaking children. As shown by other authors in this volume, this is also the case in Portuguese, Catalan, and Italian speaking children. The great importance of this sublevel lies in the fact that, for the first time, children arrive at a satisfactory solution of one of the main problems encountered during the period of the preceding level—to find an objective control of the variations in the quantity of letters needed to write any word they want to write.

Some children arrive at the syllabic hypothesis with only a quantitative control over their productions. That is, they place as many letters as syllables, but any letter for any syllable. Others arrive at the syllabic hypothesis with some knowledge about the particular letters that may be used to represent such a syllable.

Since vowels are very regular in Spanish (five letters for the five vowel phonemes), it is relatively common to find syllabic written productions that make use of these vowels in a regular way. In other cases, the selection of which letters to use is the result of the assimilation of the available information to the syllabic hypothesis.

Very often, children use the initial letters of a proper noun with a syllabic value. (For instance, the *M* of Maria becomes "the Ma," the *S* of Susana becomes "the Su," and so on.)

So, from the qualitative point of view, during the syllabic sublevel, children may start looking for similar letters in order to write similar "pieces of sound" of the words. The resulting sound-to-letter correspondence is not the conventional one. But, for the first time, children begin to understand that the written representation tied to the alphabetical writing system needs to focus almost exclusively on the sound pattern of words.

We still need careful analyses of the syllabic sublevel with English speaking children. On the basis of nonsystematic data reported by various colleagues, I would assume the following situation to be the case:

1. A syllabic hypothesis is less explored by English speaking children than by Spanish speaking ones. This is probably due to the fact that monosyllabic nouns are much more frequent in English than in Spanish. As the minimum quantity principle is not abandoned during this period, monosyllabic words (that ought to be written with only one letter, according to the syllabic hypothesis) constitute a big obstacle to the construction of a syllabic hypothesis. The best examples we have of syllabic writing in English correspond to compound nouns (such as SPM for *Superman*) or to entire sentences.

2. English speaking children frequently use their spelling knowledge, i.e., letter names as syllables of the words being written and make use of more consonants than vowels in their productions.

Constance Kamii et al. (1986) have found evidences of this kind of syllabic writing in kindergartners. One child, they reported, writes VKN for *vacation*, CMNT for *cement*, OEN for *ocean*, and PP for *pop*.

According to their findings, 46 percent of the population studied (89 children out of 192) belong to this level that they call *consonantal* instead of syllabic. I agree with these authors when they said that "Spanish is a different language from English in that it is mainly syllable-timed and English is mainly stressed-timed."

However, it seems to me that the data they report show a great similarity between these English examples and the Spanish ones: Children choose one letter for a part of a word that corresponds to more than one phoneme. Spanish speaking children prefer to use vowels (but consonants are not excluded); English speaking children prefer to use consonants (but vowels are not excluded). So, it seems misleading to speak about a *consonant level* as opposed to a *syllabic level* (equated with a vowel). More research of a truly comparative nature is needed to clarify these issues.

From the cognitive point of view, the syllabic hypothesis represents the first attempt to deal with a very important and general problem — the relationship between the whole (a written string) and the constituent parts (the letters themselves). The ordered parts of the oral word — its syllables — are put in a one-to-one correspondence with the ordered parts of the written string — its letters (Ferreiro, 1985).

As satisfactory as it could be from the point of view of the child, the syllabic hypothesis will be repeatedly invalidated externally by environmental print and by adult productions. Without abandoning this hypothesis, children begin to try out a new hypothesis, the syllabic-alphabetic, where some of the letters may still stand for syllables while others stand for smaller sound units (phonemes). This is a typical unstable solution that calls for a new constructive process.

When children finally arrive at the third sublevel, the alphabetic hypothesis, they have understood the intrinsic nature of the alphabetic system, but they still cannot deal with all the specific orthographic features of the language (such as punctuation marks, blank spaces, polygraphic representation of phonemes, and upper and lower case letters). They have just understood that similarity of sound implies similarity of letters, as well as that a difference in sound implies different letters. So they write according to this principle; namely the main principle of any alphabetical writing system. Consequently, they try to eliminate the irregularities of the orthography. They cannot deal immediately with all the graphic particularities of a given alphabetical system, because the mass of graphic features assembled under the common name *orthography* follow other rules related to other principles.

Of course, this is not the end of literacy development. As with any other level, the alphabetic level is the end point of the previous evolution and, at the same time, the starting point of new developments. Many cognitive problems have been solved at that moment. New problems will arise.

Pedagogical Implications

I would like to suggest some general pedagogical implications that emerge from our work and relate to all of the chapters in this volume.

Knowledge of the psychological evolution of the writing system by teachers, psychologists, and diagnosticians is invaluable in order to evaluate children's progress and, even more important, to "see" otherwise unnoticed signs of literacy development. The construction of new observables, whether in children or in adults, is a function of available schemes. Many things are not observable when we do not have a reliable theory to interpret them. Many things remain unnoticed if we do not have the possibility of making sense of them. Literacy development is not a matter of sounding out the letters, repeating again and again the same strings of letters on a page, or applying reading readiness tests to assure that literacy instruction begins with the guarantee of success. When teachers understand this, they begin to think differently and respond differently to children's answers, to children's questions, to children's interactions, and to children's productions. Teachers begin to discover that children are as intelligent, active, and creative in the domain of literacy as they are in math.

Knowing the psychological evolution of the writing system does not solve any of the problems teachers have in organizing classroom activities. Many practices became ridiculous when seen through the knowledge of the evolution of literacy. At the same time, the knowledge provides a sound basis to use to reject an entire set of school practices tied to a behavioristic tradition. But to reject is not enough. Teachers need to know what to do instead. Some teachers are so accustomed to asking for new methods, new materials, new tests, and so on that they sometimes start asking researchers like myself to do their job for them.

Nevertheless, I refuse to conclude my research with the production of new materials, new readiness tests, or new methods. Let me be clear. The tradition of all these "pedagogical gadgets" is behavioristic. These instructional materials are produced, organized, and administered with the idea that adults can control the learning process, that they can decide when it is time to start learning, what is easy to learn and what is difficult to learn, what is "readable," what is "teachable," and what is the right order for presenting stimuli.

Taking seriously the consequences of psychogenetic development means putting the children with their assimilation schemes at the center of the learning process—realizing that children learn in social settings and not in isolation. It means accepting that everyone in the classroom is able to read and write—each one at his or her own level, including the teacher. It also means understanding the developmental meaning of seemingly strange answers or questions and acting in accordance with the problems children face at crucial points in their development.

Sometimes teachers will give information in a direct way, sometimes in an indirect way. Sometimes teachers will stimulate conflicts; sometimes they will leave children trying to avoid conflictive situations; sometimes they will suggest alternative solutions. Yet, at all times, teachers will provide multiple occasions to learn. They will stimulate exchanges between children and will try to understand the way children are thinking, given the particular requirements children may have at specific moments of their evolution.

Knowing the psychogenesis of literacy does not imply, therefore, remaining static, waiting for the next level to appear. Particularly in developing countries, where a large part of the population is still outside the literacy community, the school has the enormous responsibility of providing children with literacy experiences that parents cannot provide.

In my opinion, it is necessary to think about school settings in terms of literacy environments and not just in terms of teaching methods (as has traditionally been the case). It is essential to reflect on the kinds of practices through which children are introduced into literacy and the way written language is presented through these practices.

More often than not, school practices present the writing system as an object of contemplation. Children can look at it and reproduce it, but they are not allowed to experiment with it or transform it. When the writing system is presented as an object of contemplation, the hidden message that is transmitted is that this object is the property of others and cannot be under the ownership of children. It is an object that has a permanent and immutable condition that cannot be transformed, altered, or recreated through social exchanges.

These are school practices that put the children outside the knowledge domain because they define the learner as a passive spectator or as a mechanical receptor. In such settings, children learn that all of their questions are irrelevant. They learn to answer without thinking and to accept without resistance. They learn that even the naive questions are out of place. For instance, even the question "Which letter is this one?" is excluded. If the letter is a new one, they must wait until the teacher decides to present it, or if it is an old one, they are supposed to know it already.

There are no neutral pedagogical practices. As Paulo Freire repeatedly says, "All educational practices are always a theory of knowledge in action." There is no escaping the necessity of reflecting on how we conceive the *object* of the knowing process and the *process of knowing* when we talk about the school.

Literacy Development and Pedagogical Implications: Evidence from the Hebrew System of Writing

T he main focus of the psychogenetic approach to literacy development is the interaction between the child and the written system. One of its main assumptions is that encounters with print are almost unavoidable. Hence, all research efforts are oriented to discern the conceptions that children construct about the written system while interacting with it and to determine whether these conceptions change as children grow.

My own research was carried out in Hebrew with my colleague, Iris Levin. Since the focus is on the interaction between the child and the written system, it will be helpful to explore some of the features of the Hebrew system of writing. Hebrew shares all the superordinate features with the Roman systems; for example, linearity, presence of distinct units, and regularity of spaces. However, Hebrew differs in its ordinate features, such as the specific shape of its units, the direction of writing and reading—from right to left—the letters in a word, and the words in a text.

Hebrew orthography consists of a consonantal skeleton that includes 22 forms. Vowels as well as accents are not indicated by graphemes but rather by a secondary marking system of little dots and tiny lines inserted beneath, above, or within the graphemes. Spacing between groups of graphemes is, as in English, the main clue for word boundaries. Every word, independent of its syntactic category, appears separated by spaces.

The intuitive definition of a word that any literate English speaker possesses is enough to grasp the Hebrew orthographic segmentation, except in the case of some prepositions and articles. In English, prepositions and articles are written as separate words, whereas in Hebrew most of the prepositions and the only existing article are written juxtaposed to the modified words. For example, in English, the phrase *in the house* has spaces between the preposition and the determiner. In Hebrew, *inthehouse* appears as a single word (_בבית_).

Another clue to segmentation between words is provided by the so-called final letters. Five letters have graphically different alternatives that appear only at the end of a word. In addition, the orthographic notation of some bound morphemes that specify gender or number, for example, also can act as clues for the end of words because their spelling is absolutely regular.

These differences between Hebrew and other written systems offer an invaluable opportunity to verify the generality of the developmental phenomena traced in children exposed to Roman systems of writing (Ferreiro, 1982a; Ferreiro & Teberosky, 1979). In the first part of this chapter, I will sketch the development of writing as it appears in a series of studies conducted in Hebrew. The readers who are familiar with the Ferreiro and Teberosky studies (1982) will have strong feelings of déjà vu. This is understandable. If children's interactions with the written system are regulated by general assimilatory schemes, then we may expect developmental regularities across orthographies, especially in the initial steps of becoming literate.

The Emergence of Writing

Our initial study explored how children's drawing and writing become mutually distinguishable and when their writing begins to look like Hebrew (Tolchinsky Landsmann & Levin, 1982, 1985). In the study, 42 children aged 3 to $5^{1}/_{2}$ were asked to draw and to write alternatively single words and short sentences. The findings indicated that very few children, and those only from the youngest age group, produced writings and drawings that were graphically indistinguishable. Before the age of 4, children's writing already appears as a linearly arranged string of distinctive units separated by regular spaces. By the age of 5, children use almost exclusively Hebrew letters (for scoring procedures, see Tolchinsky Landsmann & Levin, 1985).

Figure 1 shows the productions of three children. Looking at the graphic appearance of the productions in the upper part of Figure 1, it is impossible to distinguish the writing from the drawing. In order to recognize each of them, you have to know whether the child was asked to draw or to write or whether the child intended to write or to draw. The difficulty in defining early symbolic productions according to objective external patterns is not exclusive to the ontogenesis of writing. A similar phenomenon characterizes the emergence of other symbolic manifestations as well. A child's first spoken words are recognized not by their phonetic shape but rather by the situation in which they are pronounced. Similarly, only the conditions of productions would define a particular graphic outcome as writing or drawing.

It is much easier to recognize the drawing and the writing in the middle part of Figure 1. The writing on the right looks like writing — not necessarily like Hebrew writing — but like any writing. It is characterized by the superordinate features of a written text — the features that Hebrew shares with any other system of writing. Finally, the productions in the lower part of the figure exhibit the ordinate features of Hebrew orthography. All the graphic units the child used are conventional Hebrew letters, although they are totally unrelated to the words the child was asked to write.

In line with Gibson and Levin's (1975) description, the emergence of Hebrew writing seems to follow a path of increasing differentiation, from superordinate to ordinate features, as found in Roman systems. This movement toward the graphic features of the writing system constitutes the figurative side of the child's development of the writing system, since these graphic features are a sort of raw material on which children work out their own constraints. These constraints, as the reader will see shortly, seem to be general across orthographies.

The Regulation of Writing

The differentiation of iconic and noniconic modes of graphic representation constitutes the first period in the ontogenesis of writ-

Figure 1
Writing and Drawing of Young Children

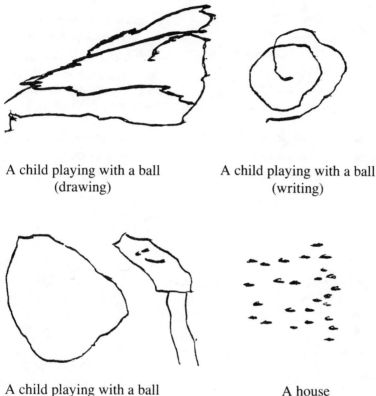

A child playing with a ball
(drawing)

A child playing with a ball
(writing)

A child playing with a ball

A house

ד,ד,דד

דאֶחֹן

ing, as described by Ferreiro. Once children start to write, the disposable space creates limits. Progress consists of organizing the graphic shapes into a line and introducing a controlled number and variety in the ordered forms. Having these two organizing principles, children will be able to look at each piece of writing and de-

Figure 2
Children's Writing Samples

Nataly
נאטאלי

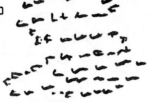

A red flower
perach adom
פרח אדום

Sky
shamaim
שמים

Inbal
ענבל

עֹרָץ

עבֿרץ

עֹנּבֿלּ

A red flower
perach adom
פרח אדום

A house
bait
בית

Sky
shamaim
שמים

Orit
אורית

יאת

יאת

אירהן

A red flower
perach adom
פרח אדום

A house
bait
בית

Sky
shamaim
שמים

30 *Tolchinsky Landsmann*

cide whether it makes sense or is only a group of letters that are not a "meaningful" written representation.

Figure 2 shows the writings of three children. Nataly's writing on the top is unconstrained and is spread over the whole page. In the case of Inbal, however, we see a drastic reduction in the number of forms used to produce what, in her view, constituted a written display. The number of characters is drastically reduced, as well as the variety. Inbal is using Hebrew letters, the letters of her own name, in a mixture of script and print. However, Inbal produced the same written string for every utterance she had been asked to write. She produced only intrawriting variations and not interwriting variations. In spite of the external similarity of all her written production, she did not hesitate to read in each of them the different words and sentences she was asked to write. Inbal is still unable to produce different writings for differences in meaning and doesn't see the contradiction of reading different messages in the same written display.

Orit, although still utilizing only the letters of her name, already is capable of producing interwriting variations—writing each word with a different arrangement of the same letters. She produced objective differences in the arrangement and in the quantity of letters to represent different words and sentences. Orit's productions already belong to what Ferreiro defines as the second level in the ontogenesis of writing (this volume). The main characteristic of this period is the production of different writings for different utterances.

Beyond a doubt, the features of the written system play an important role in the appearance of precisely these principles in children's writing. The written system possesses a finite number of graphic shapes that combine in multiple but regulated ways to produce new meanings. We should remember that this is what turns a physical/graphic manifestation into a conventionalized notational system. Nevertheless, I am still unable to explain why the children worked out precisely these constraints. In any case, the regulation of writing in terms of quantity and variety indicates the passage from graphics to symbols. The next problem children need to solve is that of the representational meaning of this notational system.

The Significance of Writing

The main characteristic of the second level in the ontogenesis of writing is the production of writings that differ in the amount or variety of letters used to represent different utterances. Certain questions relating to this level become evident to the researcher. According to which criteria, if any, are the differences among writings produced? Linguistic events are multilayered. Which layers are the children attempting to represent? Exactly what differences between utterances are they trying to tap?

As Ferreiro (this volume) suggests, children are not analyzing the sound pattern of the word but are working with the linguistic symbol as a totality (meaning plus sound). Initially, children seem to test the following hypothesis: Perhaps the variations in the quantity or variety of letters are related to variations in the quantifiable aspects of the objects to which they refer.

Let us call this hypothesis *the referential hypothesis*. The referential hypothesis establishes a relationship between language and the world. Logically, it is possible to expect a referential link to any of the features of the object. Ferreiro argues, however, that children believe that only the quantifiable features of the object are reflected in writing and that these features are reflected through a quantitative matching to the amount of letters. In other words, there are more letters for bigger, older, or more numerous objects. Ferreiro believes that the representation of shape is recognized very early as belonging to the iconic mode of representation and, as such, is rejected for written representation. Ferreiro does not refer explicitly to a referential link to other features such as color (Ferreiro & Teberosky, 1982).

Nevertheless, in our first study we found some examples of nonquantitative referential links. For instance, there were children who write the word *sky* at the upper part of the page and in blue. Vygotsky (1978) also reported a study by Luria in which children tended to reproduce in their writing the shape or color of the objects mentioned in a list of phrases. Because of this conflicting evidence, a second experiment was carried out to reexamine the referential issue (Levin & Tolchinsky Landsmann, 1989).

In the experiment, 80 children aged $5^1/_2$ and $6^1/_2$ were asked to write four pairs of words representing objects that were differentiated by a particular salient feature—shape, color, size, or quantity.

Since older children may tend to write more characters for longer sounding words, the shorter sounding word stood for the bigger or more numerous referent (*elephant/ant, pil/nemala* and *coop/chicken, lool/tarnegolet*). (In the examples, English is stated first, followed by Hebrew transliteration.) The two other pairs of words, representing shape and color differences, were each composed of two words of about the same length (*rope/ball, hevel/kadur* and *tomato/cucumber, agvania/melafefon*). Shape and color stood for qualitative features, while size and amount stood for quantitative features. The experimental design we used allowed us to determine the extent to which children's writing reflects the referential differences between words and to test whether referential links are restricted to the representation of the quantifiable features of the referent.

Figurative resemblance is indeed closer to a replica of the object and, as such, foreign to writing. In contrast, quantitative correspondences imply a sort of translation of a feature of one system (that of the referents) to another system (that of writing). Hence, we expected a shift in the use of referentialization from figurative to quantitative. We had no clear expectations regarding the use of size or color.

Almost half of the children introduced one or more referential elements in their writing. In line with our expectations, the findings showed that as children get older there is a strong decrease in the use of shape as a referential element. In contrast to Ferreiro's description, however, we found some children who, in spite of producing linearly organized strings of letters, accommodated the shape of the letters to the shape of the object they were trying to represent. We found almost no manipulation of the letters' sizes to represent the different sizes of the referents. There was an increase in the use of number of characters and a steady use of color throughout the two age groups.

Figure 3 shows the written productions of three children. In the top example, the child wrote the words *hevel* (rope) and *kadur* (ball) in a linearly organized manner with Hebrew letters. He selected, however, square, straight letters for *rope* and round letters

Figure 3
Children's Writing Shows Referential Links

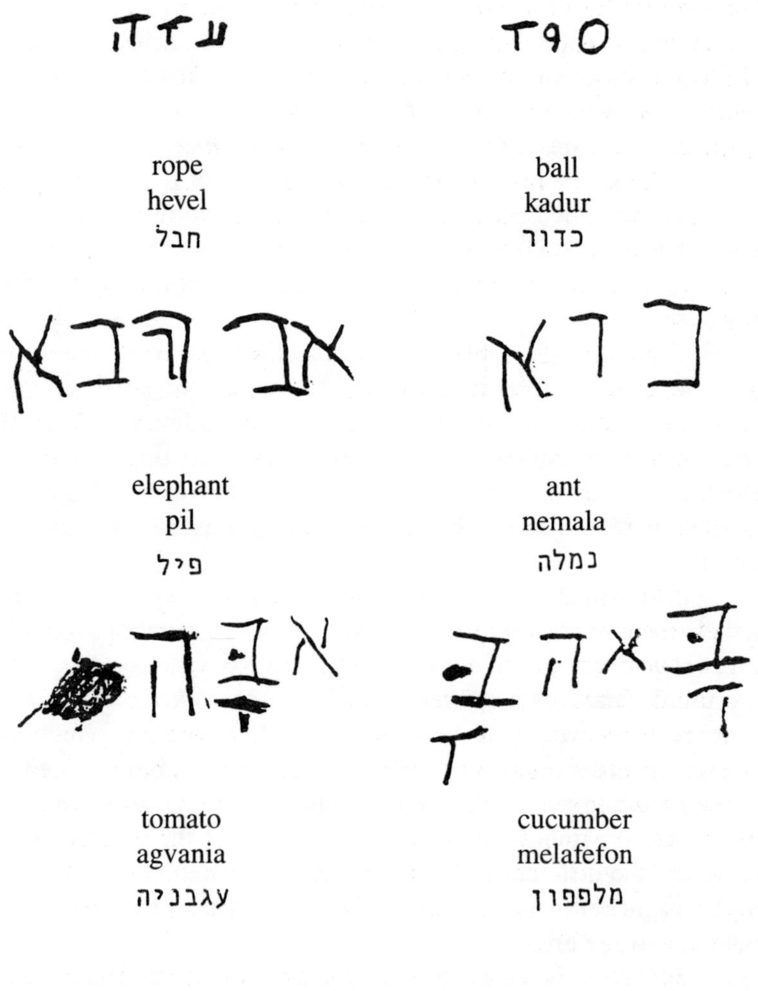

rope
hevel
חבל

ball
kadur
כדור

elephant
pil
פיל

ant
nemala
נמלה

tomato
agvania
עגבניה

cucumber
melafefon
מלפפון

for *ball*. Although cases like this were very rare, they clearly show an accommodation of the shape of the letters to the figurative features of the referents.

Tolchinsky Landsmann

The middle example in Figure 3 shows a quantitative referential link. The child represented the words *pil* (elephant) and *nemala* (ant) by writing the bigger "object" with more letters. It is important to mention here how this child read back what he had written. He segmented the words into syllables and tried to find a certain correspondence between syllabic segments and letters. He had no problem with the shorter word that he wrote, because he could segment the spoken word *nemala* (ant) into three syllables, each for a different letter.

The problem started with the longer word he had written, which he represented with five letters. In this case there was a real conflict between the number of letters and the number of oral segments. The child looked at the letters and read "pi-ll," leaving three letters without the corresponding sound value. He looked again and said, "One moment (rega) – pi-ll." This time only two letters were left without an oral "reading" rendition. The child was still not satisfied. He glanced again at the letters and then read: "pi-i-i-ll-ll." The same logic was applied to the word *lool* (coop), which was written with many more letters than the word *tarnegolet* (chicken). The conflict between the written and sound patterns was solved in a similar way. It seems rather clear that the initial guideline was referential, but the sound pattern of the word was not ignored. In other words, the child struggled between these two parameters.

The example on the bottom of Figure 3 is a qualitative referential link. The figure shows the word *agvania* (tomato), which was written in red, and the word *melafefon* (cucumber), which was written in green. In this case there was also a conflict between the writing and the sound pattern, but since the quantitative correspondences were not in question, it could be solved differently. Initially, both words were written with four Hebrew letters, the same letters in different combination. The child looked at the letters and read "ag-va-nia," segmenting the word into three syllables, although grammatically it is segmented as a four syllable word. Hence, there was a lack of correspondence between the number of letters and the number of syllables.

The child then looked at the written display and crossed out the last letter. Since the correspondence between the size of the object and the number of letters was not the established referential link, the child had no problem in modifying the number of letters. These two examples in Figure 3 illustrate that children really are struggling between the referential and the phonetic parameters of words. Sometimes these two parameters appear to be contradictory, whereas at other times, they seem to be alternative. This is reasonable, since if children are dealing with the linguistic sign as undifferentiated duality, alternative centrations in the referential parameter as well as in the sound pattern may be expected.

In any case, according to Ferreiro, during the next level the phonetic parameter will become the main guideline for children's written productions.

The Representation of Language

The third level in the ontogenesis of writing is the "phonetization of writing," i.e., the attempt to represent in writing the sound pattern of the word. We know from Ferreiro's description that initially when children "discover" phonetic representation, their unit of correspondence is the syllable. It is absolutely understandable that children start their letter/sound correspondences in terms of syllables rather than in terms of phonemes. Syllables have a reality or existence of their own. They can be pronounced in isolation, independent of the totalities into which they may be placed. In contrast, phonemes are abstract, formal. They have no existence except relative to the whole of which they are a part.

When children are asked to represent differences between words, their option is very clear. Between two meaningless units such as syllables or phonemes, they tend to opt for the syllable, which at least has *phonetic substance.* But what if they are going to represent different sentences? Are they still going to resort to meaningless units?

Based on the same developmental path according to which referential differences are represented earlier than phonetic differences, we expected that children would be able to represent the word structure of a sentence even before being able to represent the syllabic structure of a word. In order to test this expectation, we designed an experiment in which 120 preschoolers and beginning first graders were asked to write two series of utterances. The two series included four utterances each that increased in length. The longest always contained the shortest one as part of it, such as *A girl is dancing / A girl is dancing and singing very well.* (Although not all of the utterances were grammatical sentences, they will be referred to as sentences throughout.)

The two series of utterances differed in that one of them had sentences composed predominantly of verbs and adverbs (see the preceding example), while the other had sentences composed predominantly of nouns, such as *Tali and Eran are building a tower.* Consequently, in the first series we have an increment of words but not of the objects referred to; a single girl is the actor in the four sentences. In the second series, we have an increment of words and of objects.

All the written productions elicited by these series of sentences were compared in terms of number and types of characters. We did not compare the child's writing to conventional writing but instead compared each child's productions to themselves in terms of number and types of characters. These analyses allowed us to assess how children represent the differences and similarities existing between sentences. We could see whether children use more characters to write longer sounding sentences and whether they use the same characters for the same words. We also could assess the effect of syntactic categories of linguistic elements on the order of their appearance. For instance, we could see if nouns in sentences are represented earlier than verbs or adverbs.

A gradual progression emerged in the children's use of the type and number of characters for representational purposes. Five-year-olds, in more than half of their written productions, either used the same characters to indicate identical linguistic elements in the sentences or tended to increase the number of characters as the length of the sentences increased, but not both. Only in 6-year-olds was it possible to detect a simultaneous use of both repeated and longer strings of characters to represent the inclusion relationship between the sentences. We also saw a strong effect of word category on these general tendencies. The word structure of sentences containing mainly nouns (the noun-loaded sentences) was represented earlier than the word structure of sentences containing mainly verbs or adverbs (the verb-loaded sentences). (For scoring procedures, see Tolchinsky Landsmann & Levin, 1987.)

Figure 4 presents examples of three children who exemplify different milestones in these general tendencies.

Itzik's entire repertoire consists of a singe *one*. In his system, only the referential differences between sentences are reflected. He simply made the number of *ones* correspond to the number of objects mentioned in the sentences. Roy, in the second example, wrote a series of strokes and irregular shapes that display little similarity to any Hebrew letter. His writing was not even linear. In this respect, his writing was less mature than Itzik's. Nevertheless, Roy's writing seems to be influenced by the phonetic parameter. Whenever he moved from one sentence to the other, he increased the number of characters, both in the verb-loaded sentences and the noun-loaded sentences. Roy still ignored the presence of shared words in sentences.

Adi, 5 years and 11 months of age, used Hebrew letters in her writings, but did not assign them their conventional phonological value, except for writing the word *Tali*. She possesses a great repertoire of Hebrew cursive and print. However, this is not the only respect in which her writing is more mature than that of the two boys. She also managed to represent both similarities and differences between sentences. Whenever Adi moved from one word to the next, she repeated all the letters, adding one more. In this manner, she represented both the differences in length and the presence of the same word. The influence of the referential parameter is very strong even at this level. In writing the noun-loaded sentences, she matched the graphic segmentation between groups of letters to the number of objects mentioned rather than to the number of words. In the verb-loaded sentences, her writing was unsegmented. The sentence referring to one single girl is described as an unsegmented whole.

We think that the congruence between the phonetic and the semantic parameters of an utterance and the form characteristics of writing facilitates the representation of certain differences more than others. In longer written sentences referring to more objects, the

Figure 4
Children's Perceptions of the Word Structures of Sentences

Figure 4 Sentences	Itzik איציק	Roy רוי	Adi עדי
tali Tali טלי	1	[illegible]	טל
tali ve'eran Tali and Eran טלי וערן	1 1	[illegible]	טלדדד
tali ve'eran bonim migdal Tali and Eran are building a tower טלי וערן בונים מגדל	1 1 1	[illegible]	טלידד בדגדן
tali ve'eran bonim migdal ve'rekevet Tali and Eran are building a tower and a train טלי וערן בונים מגדל ורכבת	1 1 1 1	[illegible]	טלידדנדגדוקדנ
yalda A girl ילדה	1	[illegible]	הד
yalda rokedet A girl is dancing ילדה רוקדת	1	[illegible]	הדדב
yalda rokedet ve'shara A girl is dancing and singing ילדה רוקדת ושרה	1	[illegible]	הדדבשד
yalda rokedet ve'shara yafe meod A girl is dancing and singing very well ילדה רוקדת ושרה יפה מאוד	1	[illegible]	הדדבשדסמט

phonetic lengthening of the utterance coincides with the referential increment involved, and both correspond to the way the written system represents the modification, i.e., the orthographic lengthening. Hence, it is not surprising that those cases were represented more accurately by more children and at a younger age.

We also would like to refer to the different ways children interpreted their own writing of the two series of sentences. Each time the children finished writing a sentence, we asked them to read what they had written and to point to the written text as they read. The children had in mind what they had been asked to write and could see what they had just written (generally, a discontinuous string of characters). Hence, our request posited the problem of matching a verbal utterance to a discontinuous graphic display. The different ways children approached this problem, what they selected to say, and how they said it provided valuable hints about how they conceive the relationship between a spoken utterance and its written representation.

Most of the children responded to the question, "What did you write?" by a verbatim repetition of the sentences. Many children, however, produced a partial reiteration of the sentences. The children were very systematic as to which parts of the sentences they omitted when reading them back. They never forgot to repeat the nouns. However, they omitted the verb when reading back the noun-loaded sentences and the adjectives when reading back the verb-loaded sentences. The sentence *Tali and Eran are building a tower* was read "Tali, Eran, and a tower." The sentence *A girl is dancing and singing very well* was read back verbatim. Many more children repeated the verb-loaded sentences verbatim than the noun-loaded sentences.

The phenomenon of peculiar omissions when children read back a sentence was first pointed out by Ferreiro (1978) when she asked Spanish speaking children to read back a sentence of the form N + V + Det. + N (noun plus verb plus determiner plus noun): *Papa patea la pelota/ Papa kicks the ball.* The youngest children tended to omit the verb and the determiners. Only the older ones tended to include the other parts of the utterance as well. First they included the verb and only later the determiner. This reading behavior was interpreted by Ferreiro as meaning that children assume only nouns need be written, whereas other relational or functional terms do not require an independent representation.

In contrast, the findings show that the categories of words children tend to omit depend on the type of sentences they are asked to read. In those sentences where nouns constitute the meaningful core, the children tend to omit other categories such as verbs. In those cases where verbs are the meaningful core, they tend to preserve them. Hence, our argument is that children's suppositions as to what must be written are made not in terms of word category but rather in terms of what constitutes the meaningful core of a particular utterance.

Implications of Literacy Development Research

Based on the results of our theoretical and experimental research, there are four major implications for literacy development.

The first regards the possible existence of universals in writing development or, at least, the presence of developmental regularities across orthographies. There are certain phenomena in the Hebrew language that are well known from developmental analyses in Roman systems: a similar progression from superordinate to ordinate features, a passage from intra- to interrelational variations, a reduction in the number and variety of graphic forms used to produce and recognize meaningful writings, and a passage from referential to phonetical correspondences.

These regularities speak very strongly in favor of general organizational processes that are stimuli-imposed rather than stimuli-driven. This finding is crucial to educational action. If these organizational principles are strong enough to override orthographic systems, they probably override instructional methodologies as well. Therefore, some strong advice to teachers: If you can't fight them, join them.

The second implication regards the relationship between the spoken and written language. There is an old issue in linguistics as to the status of the written versus the spoken language. Since the time of Saussure (1916), it has been assumed that the spoken language is the natural language and the written language is its representation. This phonocentrism (Scinto, 1986) is not limited to treatments in linguistics but pervades both psychological and pedagogical attitudes as well. Most educators are convinced that the mastery of oral language is an absolute prerequisite to the mastery of written language.

There have been some exceptions in this line of thought, both from linguistic and psychological perspectives. A few scholars view both speech and writing as equivalent forms of language, both of which are manifestations of the linguistic system (Derrida, 1967; Hjelmslev, 1963; Jakobson & Halle, 1956). Their arguments are fundamentally based on the need to separate synchronic from diachronic facts. It is true that speech precedes writing historically, but once the two manifestations are socially available, there is no justification for considering one manifestation as more natural than the other. Even from this perspective, oral language is perceived as playing a fundamental mediating role in the early stages of written language acquisition. Only after written language develops a degree of automaticity does the mediating role of oral language diminish (Luria, 1980; Scinto, 1986).

According to our line of research, it is possible to speak of the "natural" process of written language acquisition in the same way we speak about "natural" spoken language acquisition. Mastery of the spoken language would not be a prerequisite for fostering written language, but rather the two forms would interact from the very beginning.

The third implication regards the level of language children focus on when learning to read. Many researchers and educators see the creation of associative habits linking letters to sounds as the core of learning to read (Perfetti, 1984). Chomsky (1970) demonstrates instead that orthographies tap lexical morphemic levels and preserve them across contingent variations of time and space. Our subjects seem very Chomskian in this respect, since they appear to be concerned with these levels of language from their very first involvement with reading and writing.

The fourth implication relates to the general relationship between research in developmental psychology and the applications of that research to education. Many developmental psychologists arrive at detailed descriptions of the sequence of acquisition of a particular concept in a linguistic or cognitive domain. Examples include the developmental order of the acquisition of relative clauses in linguistics or the concept of average in mathematics. Then comes the question formulated by the professionals in school settings about the possible applications of the described sequence to classroom instruction or curriculum planning.

No developmental description can provide clues for application without a hypothesized mechanism of development. There must be some hypothesis for an intervening mechanism that leads from one step of the sequence to the next one, and the pedagogical action must be inspired from this hypothesis. The major contributions of Piagetian research as applied to education are not simply in the developmental descriptions that have been generated. Piaget also provided the hypothetical mechanisms he conceived as crucial for development: the intrapersonal conflict—between existing but different assimilatory schemas, the interpersonal conflict—between different ideas regarding the same problem, and the intra and inter-confrontation between personal conceptions and socially established conventions. In addition to the above, Piaget pointed to the possibility of reflecting on one's own action as accounting for development (Piaget, 1971, 1979). Most of the experimental situations in the psychogenetic line of research were built taking into consideration these hypothetical mechanisms.

In the case of the studies cited here, children were asked to write contrasting pairs of words. The phonetic and semantic parameters of the words were usually in conflict, and the experimenter usually posed provocative questions. The children's own writings remained in front of them so that they could compare them and reflect on them.

These mechanisms that foster development lead to implications for classrooms. Several different types of texts would be preferred over a single text, and several different types of letters should be used for writing rather than only a single, designed form. Writing and reading should be viewed as group activities rather than as solitary acts of copying or sounding out.

Children need to be provided with opportunities to confront and to reflect upon their own writing and reading, to review what they do, to compare successive writings, and to contrast ideas about a particular text. Also, children prefer to work on transforming texts rather than on looking at static letters or words. In short, reading and writing must be active learning situations.

In almost every presentation of his theory, Piaget emphasized the need to see the functioning organism as active rather than passive in the acquisition of knowledge. By activity, Piaget implied not only manipulation but also mental action that transforms to create understanding.

> If every action implies assimilation and if assimilation is defined as incorporation of objects or of external links into schemes of action, every action vis-a-vis an object transforms this object in its properties and its relations (Piaget, 1958).

The role of activity as manipulation always has been emphasized in the teaching of reading and writing. Children are encouraged to build words with block letters, to write with clay or on sand, and to engage in other such activities. The role of activity as mental action that transforms something in order to understand it is a less recognized and far from accepted practice. The psychogenetic outlook on literacy emphasizes precisely that role of mental action. Children have to transform conventional systems of written language in order to understand them.

We have shown children transforming the semiotic function of writing, the rules of correspondence between graphic and linguistic units, and the rules of graphic segmentation between words. These deviations from the conventions of writing could have been interpreted as mere novice behavior. In our view, they represent real transformations for better understanding. Only by accepting this sense of the activity construct would a class situation be considered as being mentally active in the development of literacy.

Finally, most of the research that stems from the psychogenetic approach sets tasks for the child that exceed his or her knowledge and abilities, as defined by adults, in order to discover the history of knowledge. In so doing, the child is recognized as an epistemic agent — a producer of knowledge. This has to be the main feature of any pedagogical proposal focused on literacy.

4

Ana Teberosky

The Language Young Children Write: Reflections on a Learning Situation*

I n this chapter, I will explore a traditional learning activity in beginning reading and writing—writing linked to pictures. In beginning reading and writing materials, it is common to present a name or noun written in spatial proximity to a picture. (In beginning reading and writing texts in Spain, where this work was carried out, the name/noun is used without an article.) The name represents either the object as a whole or some of its parts or attributes. Attaching a whole name to its referent is a common behavior, not only in mother/child interaction while reading picture books (Ninio, 1980; Ninio & Bruner, 1978), but also in the individual processes in comprehending writing (Ferreiro, 1982b).

Ninio and Bruner (1978) found that both mothers and children named the whole object more than parts or attributes of it. From the mother's point of view, this naming behavior is a teaching task.

Studying the development of written representation, Ferreiro (1982b) finds that 3- and 4-year-old children think that the name of the image is written in the letters accompanying a picture. Ferreiro affirms that children at this age even use the term *name* to refer to the written text. The *name* would be both the written text and the content that can be attributed to it. The exclusive naming of parts, actions, or attributes of objects, without reference to the object as a whole, would seem, then, to be a school practice that does not occur in social (Ninio, 1980) or individual activities in the real world.

*Translation from the Spanish by Karen Goodman

Some authors have observed that spontaneous writing activities that develop within the family environment are suspended when children begin school (Y. Goodman, 1980, 1982) or may continue to develop outside of and parallel to school writing activities (Bissex, 1980). It is a challenge to schools, then, to organize learning situations that incorporate the spontaneous writing activities of children without inhibiting them. In doing this, it not only is possible to help children learn but also to turn the classroom into a laboratory for observing children's ideas and responses concerning written language.

In order to study such ideas and responses, it was necessary to consider pedagogical situations that simultaneously took into consideration the cultural practices of the society in relation to literacy as well as children's ideas about what is written and how things are written in their initial experiences with learning to read and write at school. The experiences discussed in this chapter took place in the Escola Municipal Casas of Barcelona. Instruction was carried out in the Catalan language. The child population was primarily Spanish-Catalan bilingual, and the original writings by the children were in Catalan.

In considering activities involving "writing with pictures," I had to decide what kind of pictures and what kind of instructions from the teacher would elicit the best responses from the children. A series of situations appeared to be good invitations for "writing with pictures." These were situations that gave rise to a list of names: proper names of the children in the class, names of the characters from a story, names of Christmas presents the children might wish for, a list of objects to take on a trip, and a list of titles of familiar stories. My concern was to get children to write names (as a grammatical category) and longer phrases, but I recognized the importance of allowing the children to have diverse models of written texts, not simply the models traditionally offered by the teacher and classmates.

In this chapter, the term *written language* refers to both the graphic aspect and the linguistic content. Blanche-Benveniste (1982) differentiates between "technical aspect" and "the language for writing." *Written language* should be understood as the "writing of language" (Ludwig, 1983; Vachek, 1982) or as "the language that is written." We have selected the latter point of view. It should be clear that this type of construction can be performed on an oral as well as a written level.

Because of the concerns for both helping the children to progress and offering them opportunities to copy, compare, and consult written models, the activities of writing with logos, ads, photographs, and newspaper texts evolved. I will present and discuss the responses to the "writing with pictures" situation from 4- to 8-year-olds, which correspond, in Spain, to the first and second year of preschool and the first, second, and third grades of elementary school education.

The Use of Ads, Newspapers, and Promotional Texts

Commercial labels are good printed material that can be used by the youngest children for learning about the writing system. Many labels appear frequently on television, in magazines, and on products consumed in the home. In addition, labels maintain a degree of constancy in their physical appearance—the same letter type, the same form, and the same color. Their continuous presence in the environment and their graphic constancy lead children to associate the overall form of the label with its text and to recognize the brand or product being advertised. The association of the product with the text of the ad can be considered the objective of the promotion.

For educational purposes, it is possible to benefit from this circumstance and invite children to write in response to commercial labels. For the youngest children, we (the teacher in the school and I) used a methodology of progressive decontextualization similar to the one used by Heath (1983). This simply consisted of getting children to use more and more textual cues at the expense of figurative ones. In the beginning, we presented the ad just as it appears in magazines or newspapers, and in subsequent presentations, the children responded only to the commercial label and its slogans.

We used the same procedure with photographs of public figures, signs seen frequently in the city, and titles and logos of children's and adults' magazines. It is interesting to note that children seem to write their own texts without attempting to copy, although they may sometimes use some letters from the commercial labels in their own productions. Eventually, they learn to copy (Dyson, 1985) as a way of "conventionalizing" their writing.

From the written responses we examined, we selected 127 of the children's productions completed over a two-month period and classified them into two broad categories: presentation and definition of the object, and persuasion for using the object (in the case of commercial products).

Labels, ads, and newspaper messages represent a variety of language that occurs commonly as written language in society. Commercial ads and newspaper texts are, in fact, highly conventional and often stereotypical, although they are not typically used in schools. However, for the purposes of this study, it was important to incorporate a wide variety of print styles in the classroom as models in order to discover how this activity evolves in the classroom.

Observation of a Classroom Activity

The teacher distributes cutouts of labels from magazines and newspaper headlines to 5-year-old children so that, in pairs, they will write ads, slogans, news, or whatever else the cutout suggests to them.

Teacher:	Choose one you know so you can write about it.
Didac-David:	Which one should we get? Only one.
David:	(Chooses the Frudesa label, a food product.) Writes *Frudesa is very good.*
Joseph-Gemma:	(Chooses Coca-Cola.) Writes: *Coke is, it's to drink* (see example).
Gemma:	(Chooses a text containing Ibiza.) Writes: *Ibiza is a country* (see example).
David-Didac:	(Chooses Scalextric, a brand of toy racing cars.) Writes: *Scalextric is for racing* (see example).

In general, the responses obtained surpass the level of simply naming/labeling the objects represented in the pictures. Although some of the compositions children write are simple labeling, there are complex responses as well. The 4-year-old group is particularly interesting. Most of them, by the end of the school year, produce a

la cocacola & Sas
Ej parrluza TOSE.

ESCALEBICT-ACAREBS

IBIZA IBIZAE

syllabic or syllabic-alphabetic type of writing (Ferreiro & Teberosky, 1979). However, there is no simple correspondence between the level of the written technical aspect and the language for writing. In fact, from the time children conceive of writing as a representation of language (Ferreiro, 1982b), it is possible to see various utterances represented in written form. The 4-year-olds provided evidence of complex written utterances represented at the syllabic level.

Types of Linguistic Constructions

In most situations, small children do not maintain the same oral utterance when they move from their intent—verbalized before writing—to the written composition and from the written composition to a later interpretation of it. However, the conservation of or change in these oral utterances is not the focus of this study. For this reason, the examples presented in this chapter include those with more or less conventional writing—those that are syllabic with conventional sound values and those that are alphabetic. The discussion will focus on the various utterances that arise from this school learning situation independently of the level of the technical writing form.

The types of oral utterances obtained in response to the different written texts presented to the children can be represented by the following seven examples:

A) Coke
B) Iberia airplane
C) Donuts that have chocolate
D) Nestle is a baby food
E) George Bush is the president of the United States
F) Aspirins are for coughs
G) Cookies are very good

Distributional analysis in syntax (Blanche-Benveniste, 1982, 1984; Blanche-Benveniste & Jeanjean, 1980; Jeanjean, 1985) was used for analyzing the utterances. These utterances include: *constructions without verbs,* as in examples A and B; *verbal-nominal constructions* (without a main verb), as in example C; and *verbal constructions,* as in examples D through G. Among the verbal constructions, the use of forms of the verb *to be* (is, are) is very common.

Types A and B; that is, nouns and noun phrases, have been documented as typical responses in the "writing with pictures" activity (Ferreiro, 1982b). Noun phrases, in addition, frequently comprise the titles of children's stories: "The Pied-Piper of Hamelin," "The Golden Rooster," "The Wizard of Oz," and "The Firebird."

In describing the types of utterances, the following abbreviations will be used: N = noun; (N + th) = noun + relative clause introduced with *that;* (N1) = noun placed in first position; and (N2) = noun placed in second position.

Type C (N + th) also is common in titles and is characteristic of how the subject of the discourse is presented in children's stories: "Once upon a time there was a girl that had...." or "Once upon a time there was a family that lived...."

Types B and C can be interpreted as determining structures of *N.* They are structures that specify the subject of the text either with a noun modifier (Iberia) or a *that* clause (that have chocolate).

Types D through G appear the same, but they are not. We find four different utterances, although three of them have the relating of two terms in common, resulting in a structure that can be characterized as N1 is N2. Actually, examples D, E, and F involve the relationship between what comes before and what comes after the verb *to be*. Example D (N1 is an N2: Nestle is a baby food) is common in didactic texts such as encyclopedias and manuals. Example E (N1 is the N2: Bush is the president...) is more common in the language of journalism and advertising. Example F (N1 is for N2: Aspirins are for coughs) has the form of characterization by use, whereas in example G the two terms being related are not made explicit.

Definitions

The utterances obtained in the "writing with pictures" activity that can be considered definitions are exemplified by types D, E, and F. In order to characterize them, I shall make use of the distinction arising from Fauconnier's (1984) concepts of *role* and *role value,* which also were used by Blanche-Benveniste (1987). Fauconnier believes that a construction of the type N1 is the N2 designates a performance in which N1 is an unfixed, or variable, representative of N2, which is the role or fixed property. In a construction of the type N1 is an N2, N2 designates a variable property, a value attributed to an N1 set as fixed.

Making use of this analysis, we have characterized our examples in the following way:

Type D   A property that designates a value is attributed to a subject. The attribution is defined by the nature of the subject. Examples of this type follow.

1. "The giraffe is a mammal" (Monica, age 8).
2. "Ibiza is a country" (Gemma, age 5).
3. "Coke is a very refreshing drink..." (J. Carlos, age 6).
4. "Julio Iglesias is a singer that lives in America" (Meri, age 6).
5. "Dali is an artist that makes a lot of paintings" (Marc, age 6).

Type E   The subject of an attribute is identified, designating a role. The assigned property is defined by looking for the identity of the subject, as shown in the examples.

6. "Nestle's Chocolate is the best in the world" (Alex, age 6).
7. "These words are things that *are people"* (Jo, age 8).
8. "The footprint is the mark of the animal's foot" (Alex, age 8).
9. "Margaret Thatcher is the most important woman in England" (Victor, age 7).
10. "Felipe Gonzalez is the president of Spain" (Laia, age 6).
11. "*Interview* is the best magazine in Spain" (Judith, age 6).

(In Catalan, example 7 belongs both to type D "that are things" and type E "that are people.")

In type E examples, the verb *to be* is a verb of equivalence (Blanche-Benveniste, 1987) between what comes before it and what comes after it. The construction can be inverted.

6. The best in the world is Nestle's Chocolate.
7. People are things that are these words.
8. The mark of the animal's foot is the footprint.
9. The most important woman in England is Margaret Thatcher.
10. The president of Spain is Felipe Gonzalez.
11. The best magazine in Spain is *Interview*.

In contrast, examples of type D do not work when they are inverted, as in example 2: A country is Ibiza.

Influencing this is whether the subject's quality is generic in a given situation. In fact, as Blanche-Benveniste (1987) affirms, this generic quality can be highlighted through the use of superlative adjectives such as "the best in the world," "the most important," "very good." In the data, N2 of type D has an indefinite article: "Coke is *a* very refreshing drink." In type E, N2 has a definite article: "Coke is *the* most refreshing drink." This explains why there is reversibility for the E and not for the D type.

In order to shift from "value" to "role," "Ibiza is a country" would have to become something like "Ibiza is the most beautiful island in Spain." We shall see this type of construction next.

Type F   The subject of an attribute is identified, designating a use, end, or particular circumstance. The definition is set in relating a fixed property to a variable referent. This type is close to type E, but not identical, as shown in the following examples.

12. Scalextric is for play racing (Didac, age 5).
13. Shampoo is good for bathing (Judith, age 5).
14. Cigarettes are for smoking (Joseph, age 5).
15. Mineral water is good for your health (Francesc, age 6).
16. Tomatoes are for eating (Miguel, age 4).
17. Safari is where animals live (Joan, age 8).
18. Safari is when they hunt animals (Joan, age 8).
19. Baby food is for little babies (Nuria, age 5).

Jeanjean (1985) reports the utterances with *when* in which *when* specifies a particular circumstance. In our data, what is characteristic of this type of utterance is the use most frequently of *for* but also of *where* and *when*.

The paradigm permits the following forms:

> N1 is   for
>   for the
>   where
>   when

This type of definition F can appear together with or separate from type G, for example, in its joint form, G + F, as follows.

3. "Coke is a very refreshing drink for babies" (Carlos, age 6).
15. "Mineral water is good for your health" (Francesc, age 6).
20. "Tobacco is very bad for smoking" (Manolo, age 6).
21. "Donuts...some round ones for eating" (Joseph, age 4).
22. "Aspirins is something that is very good for headaches" (Nuria, age 6).

Under these conditions we deem it reasonable to state that since the two paradigms can appear in conjunction, it also is possible to have a zero ($\varnothing$) occurrence of one of them. For example, a complete occurrence would be:

23. "Toothpaste is good for your teeth" (Patricia, age 5).

    A ($\varnothing$) occurrence of type G would be:

12. "Scalextric is for play racing" (Didac, age 5).

    And a ($\varnothing$) occurrence of type F would be:

24. "Cookies are very good" (Lucre, age 5).
25. "Uncarbonated Fanta is good" (Nuria, age 4).

Mireille Bilger (personal communication) has provided us with a helpful suggestion on this topic: perhaps one must consider different types of the verb *to be*. As Jeanjean (1985) suggests, there may be long forms, such as Example 23, and short forms, such as Example 12, which has a $\varnothing$ occurrence of "good" or "bad" ("N is for...."). Another type of short form is shown in 24. This type has a $\varnothing$ occurrence of "for" ("N is good" or "N is bad").

Finally, we have encountered other examples that cannot be characterized according to the types mentioned above, and we shall include them in type H, which is made up of those examples that were mixed because they involve some characteristics of the previous types (mainly F and G).

26. "Tobacco for men and women" (Javier, age 5).
27. "Shampoo for washing your hair" (Miguel, age 5).
28. "Buy caffeine-free Coke because it's good for your children" (Mireia, age 5).

Examples 26 and 27 could be included in the "is for" paradigm with a zero occurrence of the verb (acceptable in Spanish and Catalan).

Example 28 represents a *long* response with a *because* type of complement that functions as an argument concerning the goodness of the nature of the object mentioned in the first term. This type of construction is common in advertising.

All of the examples presented show that children involved in the "writing with pictures" situation attempt either an attestation of the objects represented in the picture or a clarification of the information they hold regarding these objects.

The written responses have something in common: they all testify to the general phenomenon of constructing lexicon and meaning. Bear in mind the instructions given by the teacher: "write something that goes with it" and in some cases, "write an ad" or "write some news." This task induces children to label (what is this?), to identify (who/what is it?), and to define (N1 is N2).

In a general sense, the examples are lexical assignments: labeling, specifying what has been labeled, and defining what has been labeled. However, there is a differentiation between the act of labeling (example types A, B, C) and an elaboration of what has been labeled (example types D, E, F, G, F/G). In the latter group, the examples present a relationship between two terms.

Table 1 presents a distribution of the children's responses in order to point out the presence of responses with definitions of type N1 is N2 from ages 4 and 5, and the continuity and frequency of their use through ages 7 and 8.

Table 1
Distribution of Constructions According to Type by Age

Age					Type					Total
	A	B	C	D	E	F	F/G	G	H	
4	6	4	1	3		3		3		20
5			4		4	8	2	7	6	31
6				12	6	5	1	3	2	29
7				10	9					19
8				13	11	3			1	28

The number of examples of types A, B, and C is based on one sample from the total body of examples. This type of construction is found commonly at different ages.

We agree with the conclusions of Fauconnier (1984) and Blanche-Benveniste (1987) that the relationship between terms is a role relationship or a value relationship (including the argument concerning the value) in which there is an attempt to interpret the nature of the attributes of a subject (the giraffe is a mammal) or the identity of a subject through its role (Corazon Aquino is the president of the Philippines or shampoo is for washing your hair).

In summary, types A, B, and C are examples of lexical construction by reference to figurative material (pictures). Types D, E, F, G, and H are examples of coreference or anaphoric relationships in which there is a relationship, not between name and object, but between two mental representations of the object. The second term of the relationship (nature, identity) confirms the conceptual elaboration of the first without providing new information (Blanche-Benveniste, 1984). This practice of "ostensive definition," according to Ninio's (1980) terminology, not only expresses a relationship between the objects and their names but, fundamentally, a relationship between the names themselves; that is, an essential language relationship.

Implications for the Classroom

Teachers, psychologists, and researchers involved with innovative approaches to the teaching/learning of reading and writing tend to succumb to the temptation of wondering how to get children to "advance to the next level." We tend to plan lessons to get them to achieve "the syllabic level," to "write with conventional sound value," and to "separate words." The initial curricula we developed in the area of written language had this orientation, although we always believed that the activities should be functional, considering the issue of what writing is for.

A few years of practice helped us to let go of that initial orientation and to develop some ideas that would be useful in considering how to propose a new approach to the teaching/learning of reading and writing.

Materials

In carrying out the activity of "writing with pictures," the selection of the pictures and the instructions given by the teacher directing the task are important. Some preschool materials give the child the impression that what is wanted are names for referents based on particular phonetic problems (letters or groups of letters that are to be taught by pronouncing the name).

By incorporating the graphic diversity of printed material found in the real world (and not simply using didactic classroom materials), we are creating conditions similar to those that children experience outside of school rather than attempting to control children's responses. Promotional labels, newspaper headlines, and signs also have the advantage of transmitting the message along with the medium of communication. Children from urban environments are quite capable of recognizing, identifying, and calling forth the message associated with the pictorial referent.

Other teachers we have worked with have accepted the evidence that in our society the news media and television stimulate "precocious literacy development," and these teachers have overcome their initial rejection of using news and advertising messages.

Messages

Our pedagogical concern has focused both on *how* children write and *what* they write. This has led us to be concerned with the messages that are written. We looked for messages that used conventional language with regular structures. That is why we used diverse genres such as stories (narratives), poetry, sayings, proverbs, news (informative messages), and ads with the children beginning at age 4. Early attention to the message helps children learn; focusing on the message reveals the work children do with written language.

In fact, the data presented here demonstrate the children's concern for defining vocabulary—a clear process of constructing lexicon and meaning. Our pedagogical proposal consists not only of revealing but also of facilitating this process. We believe it to be part of an important point in academic development. Although defining Coke as "a drink" may appear trivial in terms of content, it is not trivial as a formal exercise. The same formula will be used by children to define kinds of animals, parts of discourse, chemical elements, and historical figures throughout their schooling experiences.

Many authors point to the aspects of decontextualization and greater lexicalization as exclusive to written messages in contrast to oral messages. We believe it useful, in addition, to describe the procedures children employ to understand the meaning of the words in written messages.

This work suggests that children draw their conclusions not only from the written texts but also from the contexts, in their experience, in which the texts occur. Children's responses to print in their environment show not only development in awareness of the forms of the print but also an awareness of the different messages of the print and development of the ability to express those messages in their responses.

A Passage to Literacy:
Learning in a Social Context

T he work of Ferreiro and Teberosky (1979) has provided com-
pletely new foundations for psychological and educational
ideas about literacy development in children before systematic
school teaching. In this chapter we extend their theory and conclusions, which have stimulated research in many different countries.

We will describe the results of our research with 5- and 6-
year-old children. Our general aim is to eliminate the lack of communication—now existing in Italy as in most countries—between
kindergarten and primary school and build a well-articulated curriculum concerned with continuity.

The experimental program is called Educational Continuity
4-8. It introduced a continuity for school groups, curriculum, organization, and teachers, with children entering the program between
4 to 5 years of age and leaving at ages 7 to 8. At the same time, an
innovative curriculum was introduced in the humanistic and scientific areas, and teachers were carefully and continuously trained before and during the experimental program. Kindergarten and
primary school teachers worked together for the three years of the
program.

Before discussing the features of this program as it concerns
emergent literacy, we will provide background information about
emergent literacy in Italian children based on data that we gathered
and also from surveys in which the main goal has been the study of
literacy psychogenesis in different social and educational contexts.

Italian Children Facing Literacy

The background information about Italian children's literacy development comes from data collected in Rome, Florence, and a few southern Italian towns. In general, the results of the Italian research on literacy development are similar to those that have emerged from the research with Spanish speaking children. We found that both preschool and first grade children are distributed along the four levels of literacy development proposed by Ferreiro and Teberosky (1979, 1982). Although the rate of literacy acquisition can be very different, the itinerary is the same, and children construct similar rules, such as the minimum quantity of letters, the necessity of internal variation, and the syllabic hypothesis (see Ferreiro, this book).

We first will present data collected in three different contexts, using an interview similar to the one used by Ferreiro's team of researchers. Then we will give a general synopsis of the available data with some consideration of two main qualitative features: which ways of differentiation are most commonly used by presyllabic children, and which specific letters are used by Italian syllabic children when they try to write conventional sounds.

Preschool Children

Two different samples of 48 preschool children (4.1 to 6.0) were chosen in order to get strong social class differences. The low socioeconomic status (SES) children, who were attending a public "scuola materna" for children from 3 to 6 years old (Blachowicz & Pontecorvo, 1982), were drawn from very low income families, all living in a small town near Naples. The high SES children were attending a private "scuola materna" in Rome, and both their parents had university degrees.

Table 1 shows the big effect of SES on the levels of literacy development observed in the children: 52 percent of high SES children are at or above the syllabic level as compared to 10 percent of low SES children. However, this general lag of low SES children does not prevent some of them from reaching the higher levels of development. Qualitative data show that although many of them do not have the conventional repertoire of letters, they can invent original writings (see Patrizio in Figure 1) that show internal consistency.

Table 1

Literacy Development in Two Different Social Groups

	Number of high SES children	Number of low SES children
No differentiation	1 (2%)	5 (10%)
Presyllabic	22 (46%)	38 (79%)
Syllabic	13 (27%)	4 (8%)
Syllabic-alphabetic	5 (10%)	1 (2%)
Alphabetic	7 (15%)	0 (0%)
Totals	48	48

(Percentages are rounded off to nearest 1% and therefore may not equal 100%.)

Figure 1
Patrizio's Writing

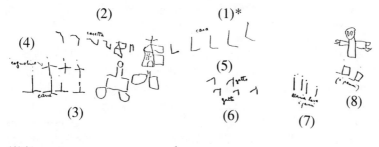

(1)*	casa	= house
(2)	casetta	= little house
(3)	cane	= dog
(4)	cagnolino	= little dog
(5)	gatto	= cat
(6)	gatti	= cats
(7)	Maria lava i panni	= Mary washes the laundry
(8)	i panni	= the laundry

*Numbers refer to words produced and indicate order of production by Patrizio.

First Grade Children

In order to test the hypothesis that entrance levels of literacy development affect subsequent learning, we studied the literacy development of first grade children in two different primary school contexts (inner city schools in Rome and a small Italian town). Children were randomly taken from many first grade classrooms in order to avoid the effects of the teachers' pedagogy.

An interesting result is that in both contexts the children, who were tested four times — October, December, March, and May — and who were at different levels during the first interview, reached almost the same literacy level by March. However, in May the children presented differences that correlated significantly to their level of conceptualization at the beginning of the year (see Figure 2).

Passage from "Scuola Materna" to Primary School

We have collected longitudinal data (over three years) with about 200 children who participated in our experimental program, Educational Continuity 4-8, as control and experimental groups. Here we can compare the differences in literacy development between the two samples (see Tables 2a and 2b), who were tested twice: once at the beginning of the first year and again during the latter half of the second year.

At the first interview, there were no significant differences in the two groups. More than 70 percent of both groups of children were not yet differentiating drawing from writing. However, by the time of the March interview, 20 children in the control group had not changed at all, and 11 children still were not differentiating after a year and a half. This is shown in Tables 2a and 2b. For example, of the 48 children who were nondifferentiating in November 1983, 10 were still nondifferentiating, 23 were presyllabic, 9 syllabic, 4 syllabic-alphabetic, and 2 alphabetic. In the experimental group, however, the evolution is striking. All of the 17 children who were nondifferentiating in 1983 differentiated drawing from writing by March 1985. Only one syllabic child did not move, and all the others moved to all levels of literacy development.

Synopsis of Our Surveys on Italian Samples

It is useful to summarize all the data that we have collected with preschool and first grade children (age range 3.9-7.2) to show

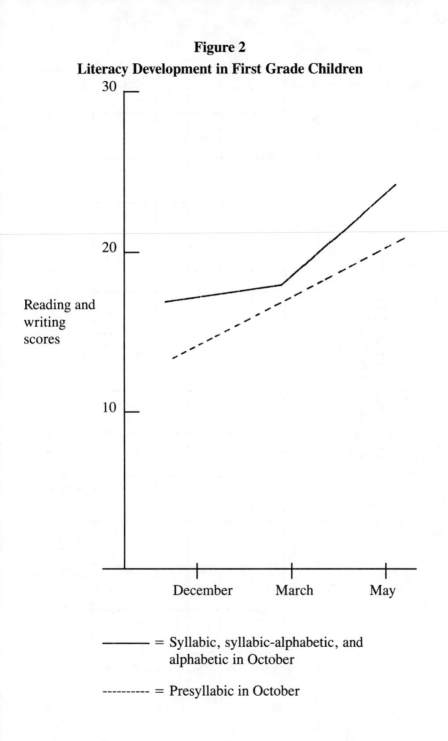

Figure 2
Literacy Development in First Grade Children

Reading and writing scores

December   March   May

———— = Syllabic, syllabic-alphabetic, and
           alphabetic in October

---------- = Presyllabic in October

Table 2
Educational Continuity: Literacy Development in Children Born in 1979

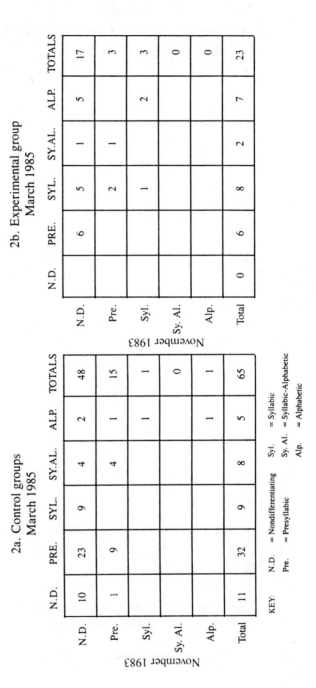

2a. Control groups
March 1985

November 1983

	N.D.	PRE.	SYL.	SY.AL.	ALP.	TOTALS
N.D.	10	23	9	4	2	48
Pre.	1	9		4	1	15
Syl.					1	1
Sy. Al.						0
Alp.					1	1
Total	11	32	9	8	5	65

2b. Experimental group
March 1985

November 1983

	N.D.	PRE.	SYL.	SY.AL.	ALP.	TOTALS
N.D.		6	5	1	5	17
Pre.			2	1		3
Syl.			1		2	3
Sy. Al.						0
Alp.						0
Total	0	6	8	2	7	23

KEY: N.D. = Nondifferentiating   Syl. = Syllabic
Pre. = Presyllabic   Sy. Al. = Syllabic-Alphabetic
Alp. = Alphabetic

Table 3
Italian Children's Literacy Development

	Materna Second Year (Age Range: 3.9-5.2)		Materna Third Year (Age Range: 5.10-6.2)		First Grade Primary (Age Range: 6.10-7.2)		
	October	March	October	March	October	December	March
No differentiation	32 (29%)	15 (47%)	7 (9%)	12 (9%)	0 (0%)	0 (0%)	2 (1%)
Presyllabic	70 (64%)	13 (41%)	57 (72%)	60 (46%)	69 (69%)	23 (23%)	8 (5%)
Syllabic	6 (6%)	4 (13%)	11 (14%)	32 (25%)	12 (12%)	3 (3%)	2 (1%)
Syllabic/ alphabetic	0 (0%)	0 (0%)	3 (4%)	9 (7%)	16 (16%)	19 (19%)	3 (2%)
Alphabetic	1 (1%)	0 (0%)	1 (1%)	17 (13%)	3 (3%)	55 (55%)	158 (91%)
Totals	109	32	79	130	100	100	173

(Percentages are rounded off to nearest 1% and therefore may not equal 100%.)

the general trend of literacy development in Italy. In Table 3, children are divided according to their school grade and the time of the year in which they were interviewed. In the seven rows, there are different subjects, with the exception of the fifth and sixth rows. It is interesting to note that there is no regular trend in literacy development and that at the beginning of the three different school years, roughly the *same* proportion of children of the three different age groups are always at the presyllabic level. This can explain the large differences found among children when they begin primary school and official literacy instruction (see the fifth row).

Qualitative Analysis

We found two main ways of differentiation (Pontecorvo & Zucchermaglio, 1988) in the writing of presyllabic children: a *formal* type of work in which the child tries—essentially through the minimum quantity and the internal variation rules (Ferreiro & Teberosky, 1979)—to control quantity and quality of signs in order to produce a diversity in writing different words, and an *external* mode of differentiation in writings in which the child changes (or keeps equal) the signifier, taking into account the characteristics of the meaning or of the referent, which is external to the writing system.

A good example of the first way is given by those children who follow the rule of a fixed quantity of letters in writing and combine them variously in order to write different words: for instance, Valeria (4.7 years old) writes RVA for "sun," OAV for "house," and IOV for "table." An example of the second way, which is less frequent, is given by Annamaria (5.7 years old), who writes "casa (house)," and "casetta (little house)" with the same letters (FIA), but uses much smaller letters for the second word (Pontecorvo, 1985).

As expected, vowels are the type of letters used mainly by our syllabic children. Most of our children use only vowels, some of them use vowels with consonants placed mainly at the beginning of the word, representing different sounds in interesting ways, and a few (and not in all their writing) use only consonants in some words. Figure 3 depicts the writing of five syllabic children, interviewed when they were in the last year of "scuola materna." Although they use many more vowels than consonants, some of them use the ap-

Figure 3

Syllabic Children with Conventional Sound Value on Vowels

Silvia: (sun) sole SLE (small dog) cagnolino AOIO
(house) casa ASA (small house) casetta AEA
(cat) gatto ATO (post cards) cartolina CTIA
Luisa: (mouse) topo OOI (post card) cartolina AOIA
(cone) cono OO+ (child) bambino AOIO
(apple) mela AIA (small dog) cagnolino
(house) casa ASI (small house) casetta ISA
Damiano: (cone) cono OO (to drink always) bere sempre
EEEE
(king) re EE (mouse) topo OO
(table) tavolo AOO (tea) te ET
(cat) gatto AO (large sun umbrella) ombrellone
OEOE
(house) casa AA
Giordano: (tower) torre OEI (queen) regina RGA
(fairy) fata ALA (horse) cavalle AAL
(dogs) cani AI (horse rider) cavaliere AALE
(dwarfs) nani AI (enchantment) incantesimo
LAEIO
(shovel) pala AL (hair) pelo LI
Mario: (cat) gatto ZO (small house) casetta ZZA
(dog) cane ZIE (large sun umbrella) ombrellone
OEOE
(mouse) topo OO (child) bambino NIO
(dinner) cena EA (table) tavolo AVO
(sun) sole OE (house) casa ZA

propriate consonants at the beginning of some words, as in the case of Silvia and Giordano. Others (as Mario) use the same consonant (Z) to represent related sounds. The writings of Damiano, who is syllabic and uses only vowels, are noteworthy. He is not following the "principle of internal variation" (Ferreiro & Teberosky, 1979), nor is he worrying about using the same letters for different words, and he accepts our challenge by writing a phrase with four Es.

The Research Framework:
Theoretical and Methodological Aspects

Our main interest is the study of children's cognition in which an object of knowledge is built in the social context of school with the active contribution of each individual child and through the social interaction that develops between the teacher and children and between peers. Our interest is to keep together *subjects* (children) and *objects* (curriculum), considering educational possibilities and social interactions between subjects, including the teacher.

From an educational point of view, we consequently consider three central aspects.

1. *The child.* The child is building knowledge with his or her cognitive and emotional means, in which metacognitive skills play an important role. It is important to assess the child's initial level of competence, since effective use of educational experience is very much linked to it.

2. *The objects of knowledge.* In this case the object of knowledge is written language, for which it is essential to have well-grounded ideas about its structural, functional, and social features. Every object of educational transmission has specific epistemological and sociocultural features that must be taken into consideration.

3. *Knowledge construction and transmission.* Much of this occurs in a context of social interactions. We include in the context of social interactions not only the educational means by which the teacher tries to transmit knowledge and to develop children's skills, but also the school environment, the norms and values of the group, the knowledge and education of the teacher (and of the children), the opportunities for communication and exchange offered to the children, and the recognition that everyone can teach (including the children) and learn (including the teacher).

Thus, combining a Piagetian with a Vygotskian approach, we consider the individual child as actively building his or her knowledge, interacting both with others and with the objects of knowledge and developing his or her organized schemes and skills through the "facilitations" offered by teachers and peers as affirmed by Vygotsky (1978).

Three General Principles

Consequently, three general principles guide our educational work: (1) preliminary and continuous analysis of the "object of knowledge" (in this case written language, with its specific features) from a linguistic, sociocultural, and cognitive point of view; (2) careful consideration of children's levels, planning activities in order to bring them to the "growing edge" (Bruner, 1986) of their competence; and (3) use of the whole social interaction network that can be developed in school and classroom contexts.

The third principle offers the main methodological aspect of our proposal. In fact, we had a double interest in using the social interaction as an educational means: it provides the context in which it is possible to study the processes of literacy psychogenesis, focusing on some particular problems that children have to face; and social interaction with teachers and peers is a powerful facilitating factor for written language development, in which the cognitive and metacognitive skills are considered central.

We used, as a point of reference, a model of social interaction that we have developed (Pontecorvo, 1986) in which we try to put together Piagetian and Vygotskian approaches to get a better understanding of the types and functions of social interaction between children and between adults and children for cognitive and social development. It results from the interaction of two dimensions with two values in each.

1. *The type of social support system.* Support can be offered by agreement, which produces coconstruction, or disagreement, which produces conflict and argumentation. We consider both the expression of agreement and disagreement as forms of cooperation, as they are forms of the social support system represented by others (Bruner, 1986). Cognitively speaking, opposition supports as much as it offers resistance, as the air does for the flying bird.

2. *The type of relationships.* These can be: asymmetrical — between expert (the teacher or a more expert peer) and novice — or symmetrical — between peers who have the same knowledge or competence.

The interaction of these two dimensions, the type of social support system and the type of relationships, produce four conditions. As shown in Figure 4, they are tutoring, coconstructing, conflict, and arguing. First we will define each of these conditions from a general point of view and, in the subsequent sections, will give examples of the different conditions within a literacy development context.

Tutoring   An adult or a more expert peer (Vygotsky, 1978) supports the cognitive work of the child, focusing his or her attention on the main points, scaffolding toward solution.

Coconstructing   A term drawn from Damon (1984) that indicates the way in which children, as we found in our previous research (Pontecorvo, 1986, 1987), put together the "pieces" of their individual mental work, building up their knowledge in the discourse process.

Conflict   The teacher tries to produce a cognitive conflict in the child by offering the child conflicting data or points of view in order to produce a change in the child's representations.

Arguing   An opposition is transformed in a dispute through specific moves (Eisenberg & Garvey, 1981; Genishi & Di Paolo, 1982), and the sequence of contrasting supports brought on by peers can develop the collective reasoning toward higher processes and outcomes.

A Curriculum for Beginning Literacy

Guided by the general theoretical framework described earlier, we developed a written language curriculum for the younger, preliterate subjects of our experimental group who were still within the syllabic level at the end of the previous year. From an institutional point of view, they were in their second year of "scuola materna" (in the second year of our experimental program of Educational Continuity), and their average age was 5.5 years.

Figure 4
A Model of Social Interaction

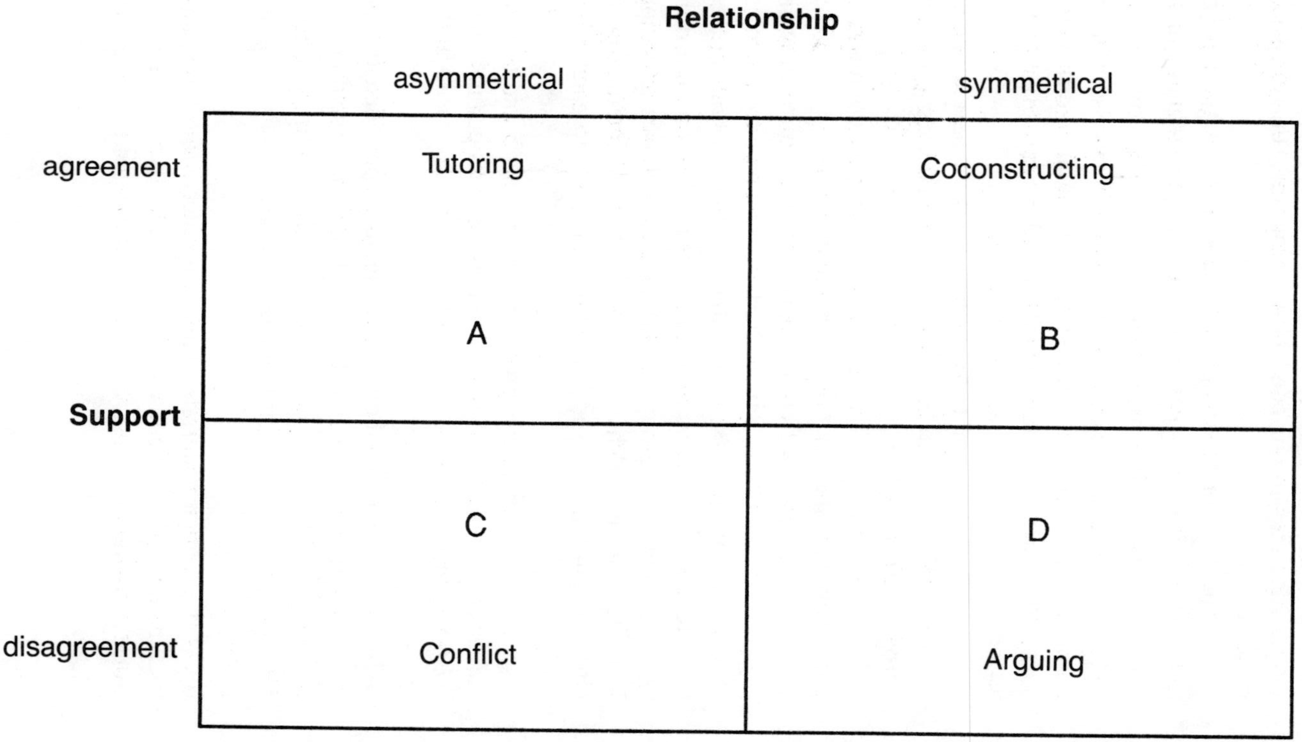

Relationship

	asymmetrical	symmetrical
agreement	Tutoring **A**	Coconstructing **B**
Support		
disagreement	Conflict **C**	Arguing **D**

Methodological Features

Besides stressing social interaction, there were two methodological features in our educational program that were specifically linked to literacy.

The first methodological feature involves the teacher's attitude toward children's learning about written language and can be expressed in the following points.

1. The teacher is not the only depository of written language knowledge (Ferreiro, 1983, personal communication), and there is a lot of "expertise" in children that must be assessed and considered as the starting point for any intervention.

2. It is important to look carefully at the developmental processes of children and to be sensitive to them during verbal and nonverbal interaction.

3. Literacy psychogenesis is a complex cognitive and linguistic process and not a purely perceptual one.

4. There are different "social practices" of reading and writing (Petrucci, 1978) to which children must be introduced early.

5. There are large variations in children both in the time it takes for their development and in their motivation toward literacy.

6. The peer group can be used as a source and support for learning, and the teacher can model a type of interaction in which children can learn to speak together and to help each other effectively.

7. The mixed age group (children ages 5 and 6 in the same classroom) can be used for enhancing the competence of all, both the tutors and the tutees.

The second methodological feature, provided by the classroom materials and organization that had to be structured in order to offer the child an adequate informational environment (Gough, 1972) in terms of written language, can be related to the following points:

1. written materials, mainly produced within the classroom, such as large double entry tablets with children's names and dates; stories invented by children about drawings or pictures, with texts

dictated to teachers; writings of the names of stores and of some familiar streets; and well-known advertising announcements;

2. labels on drawers (or furniture) in which objects are ordered and classified;

3. a reading corner as a pleasant classroom library, with a large range of books, magazines, newspapers, and texts produced by children; and

4. a writing corner, with sets of letters and numbers, papers, pens, pencils, and a typewriter.

This type of environment gives children the opportunity to exercise their skills and to reflect on written language in different "microworlds."

Since the program we present is the result of the educational experimentation, it must be stressed that we have not strictly tested its effectiveness. Rather, we have worked in the experimental school setting as a situation from which it was possible to draw data useful for an early literacy curriculum. This process can be summarized through the scheme shown in Figure 5. Although we began proposing to the teachers a curriculum that also served as a basis for their training, we want to stress that the articulated and specified curriculum is the result of the first draft implementation that was observed and discussed within the research group and with the teachers.

Curriculum Content

Our written language curriculum is founded on two main criteria: to continuously carry out reading and writing activities at two vantage points, given by the teacher and by the child's knowledge; and to differentiate work on reading from that on writing.

The adult point of view is offered by the teacher, who mediates reading and writing to the child. The teacher reads texts and writes down texts composed by the children. Allowing children to participate in the whole processes of text comprehension and composition (much before the children are able to develop the processes autonomously) operates as a strong top-down support, giving meaning to written language learning.

Figure 5
The Curriculum Development Process

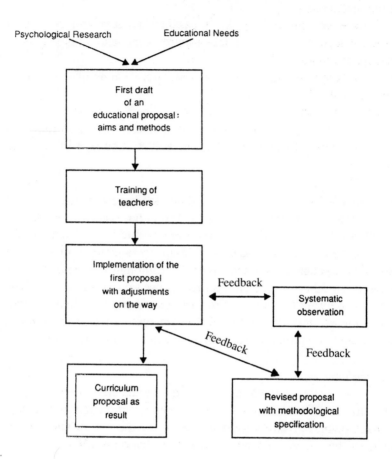

Pontecorvo and Zucchermaglio

From the child's vantage point, writing instruction starts from the conceptualization level of the child, while reading instruction takes into account the strategies with which the child gives meaning to the printed text. Taking into account the differences between the two processes, the differentiation between reading and writing is made particularly striking in beginning literacy.

Actually, a very first step in reading is to look for the meaning of writings by using almost exclusively their context: it is a top-down (Childs & Greenfield, 1980) process to focus on the global search for meaning. On the contrary, the early efforts of the child involving his or her spontaneous writing constructions are mainly formal and analytical, in which there is a search for correspondence rules and regularities without focusing (or seldom focusing) on the link to the meaning.

A general presentation of five different fields in which the curriculum is articulated, indicating the four main dimensions on which the teachers could focus their work, is given in Figure 6.

We will now suggest a few specifications about those different fields in order to explicate our linguistic and educational choices.

1. *Uses of and reflections on oral language.* Literacy learning requires general linguistic competence, which is essential, particularly for:

- vocabulary development (Thorndike, 1973/1974),
- morpho-syntactic knowledge,
- knowledge of language functions and registers,
- metalinguistic awareness (Grieve, Tumner, & Pratt, 1983), and
- decontextualized language use (Donaldson, 1978).

Consequently, a good proportion of school time was given to conversations and metalinguistic games, considered as "oral preparation to literacy" (Michaels & Collins, 1984).

2. *Writing construction and interpretation.* With the awareness that all children "write," although not conventionally (Ferreiro & Teberosky, 1979), we used the following methodology:

- to allow the children to write and to value their writings,
- to give the teachers the opportunity to assess the child's construction level and to adapt their instruction to it, and
- to let the child "read" his or her writing in order to inform the teacher about his or her symbolic level and to foster the child's awareness of his or her construction modes.

3. *Text composition.* Text composition is done without the transcription burden: a single child or a group of children produce a text that is dictated to the teacher or to a "literate" peer (Pontecorvo & Zucchermaglio, 1986).

The text can be a message, a letter, a story, or a sequential book (the morning book, the night book, and so on). Differences between oral and written language are stressed (Chafe, 1979; Ochs, 1979; Olson & Hildyard, 1985; Tannen, 1982) as much as the communicability to a reader.

4. *Early reading.* Early reading is carried out with more and more complex writing. Children are required to look for the meaning of the writing in a text or in a context that gives meaningful cues, so that they can use their linguistic knowledge (lexical and morphosyntactic) and world knowledge. The general aim is to develop the expectation that writing means something and that reading always involves understanding meaning (Smith, 1973, 1977).

5. *Text Comprehension.* Texts that differ greatly in their functions and structures (stories, tales, texts produced by children, checklists, recipes, postcards, invitations, advice, and TV programs) are read by the teachers. Children are exposed to "real" written language and not to the "artificial" books used for "learning to read" (Bettelheim & Zelan, 1982; Ferreiro & Teberosky, 1979; Lerner de Zunino, 1982). Differences in functions and registers were emphasized, as well as differences between oral and written language (Smith, 1977).

Towards Literacy through Social Interaction

Based on the previous explanations, we now will focus our attention only on two of the five curriculum fields: writing construction and interpretation and text composition (see Figure 6).

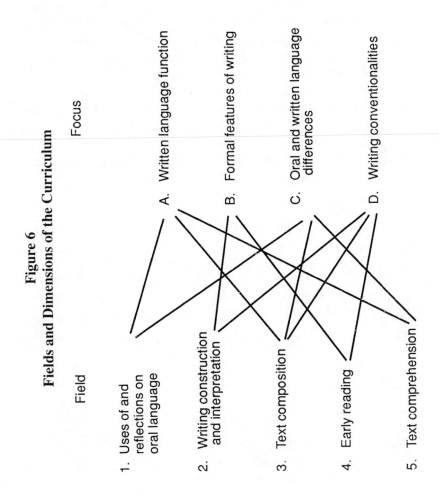

Figure 6
Fields and Dimensions of the Curriculum

Field

Focus

A. Written language function

B. Formal features of writing

C. Oral and written language differences

D. Writing conventionalities

1. Uses of and reflections on oral language

2. Writing construction and interpretation

3. Text composition

4. Early reading

5. Text comprehension

Learning in a Social Context

77

We will examine the explicit and ordered educational objectives that the teacher followed in carrying out these activities and that were the object of the teacher training (see Figure 5).

Objectives are progressively ordered from the most elementary to the most complex ones; the teacher's choice of the objective depends on the level of the child's competence. For example, the teacher introduces the more complex objective when the child shows he or she has the knowledge to participate.

Our aim is to show the different modes of social interaction that can take place in an educational setting aimed at literacy acquisition. Thus we will distinguish between adult-child interaction and child-child interaction, although in the first type of interaction there were also other children, and in the second there was always an adult.

Adult-Child Interaction

Implementing objectives for writing construction. During the time when writing construction was occurring, the teacher was working with a small group of three to four children for about 30 minutes. Groups were somewhat heterogeneous (in terms of literacy levels) in order to have diversity in the modes of writing construction but not to prevent internal communication. The activity often began by asking the children to write their own names, with the aim of motivating them to discuss different ways of construction. Table 4 shows a summarized account of the objectives proposed to the teacher.

Table 4

Objectives for Writing Construction and Interpretation Activity

1. To encourage children to produce writing, accepting non-conventional forms.
2. To ask the children to read their writings in order to demonstrate their modes of construction and to allow comparison with other children's modes.
3. To present openly problematic situations that pose a new

problem to the child, or to contrast his or her rule to the rule of others.

4. To let children recognize and become progressively aware of problems existing in their personal writing system.
5. To give support to construction problems by presenting letters in the environment, by focusing on the number of letters or the interpretation mode using task scaffolding.
6. To support the solution of more complex writing problems, offering direct or indirect information through which the children can operate at the "growing edge" of their competence.

The example that follows in Text 1 shows the variety of objectives pursued by a teacher (T) who is sensitive to the different levels of competence of the three children. With Giulio (G), she tries to intervene on the problem of awareness (objective 4) of the child (lines 29-32). With Katia (K), she poses the problems (objective 3) without going on when Katia (line 49) shows that her attention is not on the correspondence between sound and writing. With Piero (P), the teacher stops at the second objective (objective 2), since he is still producing a "global" reading of his name (line 64).

We will use the following conventions in all the text examples of the reading and writing activities of the children.

- capital letters in parentheses: any written text—word or letter—which is pointed at during reading or verbal interaction—(PIERO);
- capital letters underlined: when the text is written at that moment—<u>PIERO</u>;
- print between two / /: what is said as a result of a reading activity (of any type), of text composition planning, or of rereading—/giu/.

The first and third situations frequently occur together. For instance, in Text 1 in utterance 14, "/giu/(G)/li/(I)/o/(U)" means that Giulio pronounced certain syllables and pointed at specific letters represented by capital letters between parentheses.

Text 1

1. **T:** *Allora questi bimbi sui fogli sai che scriveranno? Il nome!* (Then, do you know what those children will write on those sheets? Their name!)

2. **G:** *Solo il nome?* (Only the name?)

3. **T:** *Il nome... cominciamo a scrivere il nome... cosi almeno ci ricordiamo.* (The name... let us begin writing the name... so at least we remember it.)

4. **G:** *E poi?* (And then?)

5. **T:** *Ehhhhhh... poi vediamo.* (Ah... after we will see.)

6. **P:** <u>*PIERO*</u> (1)

7. **K:** <u>*KATIA*</u> *Ecco!* (Done!)

8. **G:** <u>*GIULIO*</u> *Io ho gi fatto!* (I have already done it!)

9. **T:** *Benissimo! Guarda come siete bravi a scrivere il nome... Giulio, Giulio, me lo leggi il tuo nome?* (Very well! You are very good in writing your name... Giulio, Giulio. Will you read your name for me?)

10. **G:** */giu/lio/lio/* (he points at letters randomly) */Giu/(G)/lio/ (O)*

11. **T:** *Adesso me lo legge Katia il suo nome.* (Now Katia will read her name to me.)

12. **G:** */lio/.../lio*

13. **T:** *Come? Come? Scusa, eh, Giulio rileggimelo un po' bene, perchè mi sembra che ci stavi ripensando.* (How is it? How is it? Please, Giulio, would you read it again, because it seems that you are thinking it over.)

14. **G:** */giu/(G)/li/(I)/o/(U)*

15. **T:** *Eh... te ne avanzano?* (Ah... you have some more of them?)

16. **G:** *Sì.* (Yes.)

17. **T:** *Avanzano delle lettere... eh... ma è tutto il tuo nome questo?* (There are some more letters... eh... but is this all your name?)

18. **G:** *Sì.* (Yes.)

19. **T:** *Che cè scritto qui (GIULIO)?* (What is written here?)

20. **G:** */Giulio/(GIULIO)*

21. **T:** *Allora leggimelo bene adesso.* (Now show me how well you can read it.)

22.   G: */giu/(G)/li/(I)/o/(U)... /o/(L)... non ci capisco niente!* (I can't understand anything!)

23.   T: *Non ci capisci niente?* (You can't understand anything?)

24.   G: *Ma perchè mi ha scritto questo nome mamma? Me poteva chiamare in un altro modo!* (But why has mommy written this name for me? She could have called me in another way!)

25.   T: *E come ti poteva chiamare?* (And how could she call you?)

26.   G: *Da piccolo mi ha chiamato in un altro modo, invece adesso ne ha pensato un altro.* (When I was a baby she called me differently, but now she has thought of another name.)

27.   T: *Ne ha pensato un altro... e da piccolo come ti ha chiamato con un altro nome?* (She has thought of another... and when you were a baby, what was the other name that she called you?)

28.   G: *Non me ricordo.* (I can't remember.)

29.   T: *Comunque qui che cè scritto? Scusami Giulio!* (However, what is written here? Please, Giulio!)

30.   G: */giu/(G)/li/(I)/o/(U)*

31.   T: *E queste qua (LIO) che sono?* (And what are these?)

32.   G: *Ehhh... /giu/(G)/li/(I)/o/(U)...* (Giulio tries many times.)

33.   K: (laughing): *Ahh... /giu/li/o/*

34.   T: *Vediamo un po' Katia... Vediamo un po' Katia... Katia mi vuoi leggere per favore il tuo nome.* (Let us see Katia... let us see Katia... Katia, would you please read your name?)

35.   K: */Ka/(K)/ti/(A)/i/(T)/i/(I)/a/(A)*

36.   T: *Dove è /i/? Dove è?* (Where is /i/? Where is it?)

37.   K: */i/? Eccolo (I)* (Here it is!)

38.   G: */ca/(K)/ti/(A)/a/(T)... ha scritto...* (She has written it.)

39.   T: *Allora leggilo di nuovo bene Katia.* (Now, show me how well you can read it again, Katia.)

40.   K: */ca/(K)... no... /ca/(KA)/ti/(T)/i/(I)/a/(A)...* (Katia self-corrects.)

41.   T: *uhm... vedi un po' come è.* (Uhm... Let us see how it is.)

42. G: /giu/li/o

43. K: XXXXXXXX (not understandable)

44. T: *Riprova a leggerlo.* (Try to read it again.)

45. K: /ca/(KA)/ti/(T)/i/(I)/a/(A)...

46. T: *Fammi leggere... fammi.* (Read it for me.)

47. K: /ca/(K)/ti/(A)/i/(T)/a/(I)... /a/(A)

48. T: *Così?* (In this way?)

49. K: *Ci devo fare due /a/ perchè io mi chiamo /Katia/.* (I have to put two /a's/ because my name is Katia.)

50. T: *Certo, dove sono le due /a/... me le indichi?* (That's true, where are the two /a's/?)

51. K: *(A)... e (A) Eccole!* (Here they are!)

52. T: *Una e ecco l'altra... certo adesso andiamo a vedere Piero (Ada si sposta) ... andiamo a verdere Piero... che anche lui si è scritto il suo nome. Piero, me lo leggi per favore?* (One and the other... Now let us go to see Piero (teacher moves)... let us see Piero... he too has written his name.)

53. P: *Io ho scritto male...* (I have done it badly.) (Piero erases the writing.)

54. T: *Piero, me lo leggi per favore?... eh lo cancelli Piero?* (Piero, would you read it for me? Eh... are you erasing it?)

55. G: *Ha sbagliato?* (Has he made a mistake?)

56. T: *No, lo vuole scrivere con il rosso forse... vero Piero? Allora Piero leggimi il tuo nome.* (No, he wants to write it with the red color, perhaps. Is that true, Piero? (Piero is rewriting.) Now Piero, read your name to me.)

57. P: *Ho scritto questo (PIERO).* (I have written it.)

58. T: *Cosa hai scritto qui (PIERO) eh, Piero?* (What have you written here, eh Piero?)

59. K: *Eh! Quando andiamo a mangiare?* (Eh! When are we going to eat?)

60. T: *Dopo...* (After...)

61. G: *Eh, a mangiare,' ce siamo già andati... ah no!* (Eh, we have already eaten... ah no!)

62. T: *Piero...*

63.　　P: */piero/*(PIERO)
64.　　T: */piero/ dove? Tutto quanto vediamo... leggimelo piano, piano... Piero me lo leggi piano, piano?* (/piero/ Where is it? Let us all see it... read it slowly, slowly... (Piero makes a circle around his writing.)... Piero, will you read it for me, very slowly?)
65.　　P: */piero/* (Piero) (He gives a global reading of his name.)

Since Text 1 is only a selection from the teacher strategies, Figure 7 summarizes the sequence of objectives the teacher followed during the whole session. The objectives are ordered on the y axis, and the transcript progression is represented on the x axis by the number of the utterance. The teacher tries, when possible, to pursue the more complex objectives but must also adapt the activity to the children's level; the movements up and down from one objective to another correspond to the different type of work she has to do with the children.

Implementing objectives for text composition. The focus on text composition has been developed mainly in two settings.

1. Individual text composition in the classroom context: a "book of the day" was produced for every child through dictation to the teacher. The other children were working at the same time on their own books (making illustrations, writing autonomously, preparing the "index," and so on).

2. Collective text composition: a group of five or six children composed a story together using illustrations from magazines. The whole group was involved in the composition, although each child participated in developing a piece of the story.

Each of the following objectives for text composition is followed by a short example of the way the objective was implemented by the teacher (T).

1. To have the children produce elements for an expository text, building on a figurative input and starting with a descriptive analysis. [Francesca (F), Claudio (C), Fabio (Fa), Silvia (S)]

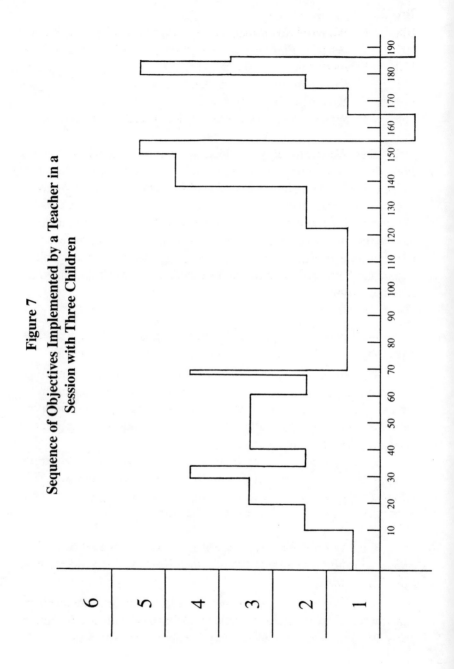

Figure 7

Sequence of Objectives Implemented by a Teacher in a Session with Three Children

Pontecorvo and Zucchermaglio

Text 2

108.	F:	We write down /bed/
109.	T:	What?
110.	F:	/bed/
111.	T:	/bed/? We write down /bed/?
112.	F:	Yes.
113.	T:	What else can we write?
114.	C:	But no! You have to write a story!
115.	T:	We have to write a story.
116.	F:	/bed when the girl arrived/
117.	T:	/On the bed/?
118.	Fa:	May I do it?
119.	S:	Do you want to cut this bottle?
120.	F:	/that the girl arrived/
121.	T:	Ah, then... /on the bed/?
122.	F:	/When the girl arrived xxxxxx/
123.	T:	What?
124.	F:	/This turned/
125.	T:	It turned... Ah beautiful! This is a turning bed, isn't it, Francesca?
126.	F:	/and it was broken/
127.	T:	It is a divan-bed then!
128.	F:	But broken...

Acting as a conversational partner, the teacher succeeds in developing Francesca's one-word proposal into an expository form.

2. To develop the elements proposed when the child asks for explanations and developments, mirroring the more productive elements that can compose a text. [Gaia (Ga)]

Text 3

69.	T:	Then... then...
70.	K:	And instead this is Gaia who comes with me.
71.	T:	Gaia, who comes with you... But Gaia comes with you where we are in the "circle," or are you the only one to stand up?
72.	K:	No... she is only accompanying me.

73. Ga: No, perhaps because I also go pee with her!
74. T: Ah, you also go pee!
75. K: Gaia comes with me. She gives me her hand.
76. T: Ah, very well... let us write down /when the children/. What else can we write?

3. To transform the child's text with the child into a written expository text by reading the previous parts in order to let the child evaluate and change them.

Text 4

166. T: What did we put down?
167. C: AZ Green. (It is a toothpaste.)
168. T: Then I will write down... then, listen (she reads) /Claudio washes his teeth with Fabio, Silvia, and AZ Green/.
169. C: No! /with the toothpaste named AZ Green/.

4. To develop the text while producing it, rereading the previous parts, asking for explanations, using the other children as audience. [Giorgio (Gi)]

Text 5

382. Gi: The end.
383. T: The end?... But do you think it is finished? (she reads) /When I went to Marco's house (I went there only once)/ ... What happened when you went to Marco's house?
384. Gi: Nothing.
385. T: Excuse me... well... it doesn't come out a sentence... (she reads again)... What happened in Marco's house?
386. S: You should say /I had a good time/.
387. T: Listen to Silvia!
388. S: /I had a good time/ ... if you had a good time, you write this way, otherwise to say... if you didn't have a good time, say that you didn't have a good time, right?
389. T: Eh! If you have played... have you?... So...
390. S: If you liked Marco's house...

391. T: Marco's company...
392. Gi: I liked it but since he had only one toy, I didn't like it. I liked Claudio's house more.
393. T: Ah, I understand... then...

5. To let the child keep the coherence between what is already in the text and what is still in progress.

Text 6

160. T: ...Then /When she arrived/ now we put in... about the computer... How could we link it to this story of the girl?... (she reads again) /On the divan-bed the girl laid down when she arrived/ and now let us see...
161. C: /And after she had to study/.
162. T: Eh, /and after she had to study/ now we will write it down (teacher writes).
163. C: I'll put it up! (He puts up the picture of the computer.)
164. T: Wonderful... what was she studying with?
165. C: /with the magic computer/.
166. T: Eh, well... /and after she had to study/ with the magic computer/ (teacher writes).

6. To insert – during the transcription of the text – analysis and reflection on orthographic conventionalities, probing children's ideas on how to transcribe intonations.

Text 7

251. T: Then... (she reads) /Giorgio says to mommy/...
252. Gi: /May I go to grandmama?/
253. T: (Teacher writes) / May I go to grandmama/ ... We put the words between quotation marks and we have to put a question mark, don't we? Because this is a question that you said, isn't it? /May I go to grandmama?/ ... (teacher reads again) /Giorgio says to mommy: "May I go to grandmama?"/
254. Gi: /Mommy says yes almost always/.

Child-Child Interaction:
Tutoring, Coconstruction, Argumentation
In giving examples of the different types of child-child inter-action, we need to discuss peer interaction in the educational con-text. We stressed (during teacher training sessions) the educational value of peer interaction for the whole experimental curriculum, re-lying on research findings (mainly grounded in Piagetian and Vygotskian paradigms) that show the positive cognitive effects of social interaction. We also were particularly aware of the emotional value of interaction, since the group can share the psychic pain of thinking and learning by dividing the problem among its members (Pontecorvo, 1987).

Furthermore, in this particular context, there was a strong stress on the social rule of helping each other as a pervasive princi-ple. It was mainly an implicitly accepted rule, although sometimes the teachers explicitly invited children to help one another. Our hy-pothesis is that the rule concerned with helping each other was pro-gressively internalized by children, who became more autonomous in using each other as sources of information and help. It seems that there is development in children—taking into account how they dif-fer in being dependent/independent from teacher evaluation—in co-operating both by supporting and by disputing one another (Zucchermaglio & Formisano, 1986).

Moreover, there are also effects linked to the task require-ments that can partly explain what type of peer interaction is most likely and most effective. Continuing to use examples from the two curriculum fields of writing construction and interpretation and text composition, we can say that it is more likely to find productive coconstruction (case B of Figure 4) in text composition activities. Conversely, it is more likely to find productive tutoring (case A of Figure 4) in writing construction and interpretation.

Argumentation was more easily produced during text compo-sition, depending on whether the child's world knowledge and social competence allowed him or her to resist the other children's ideas with good arguments. On the other hand, during writing construc-tion—although we gave the teacher the explicit objective of eliciting problems between different children's writing systems—proper comparison and subsequent conflict were effectively sustained by the child only if children were both at syllabic levels and/or their relative differences of literacy development were not too large.

Interactions in text composition. Before giving specific examples, it is interesting to focus on the ways in which children support peers on a socioemotional and motivational plane (Text 8).

Text 8

310. T: There is only one page lacking /Katia who comes back home/.
311. S: May I go to the bathroom?
312. T: Could you wait a while?
313. K: That's enough! Enough! This tomorrow!... This...
314. T: No, I am sorry, tomorrow I...
315. S: Listen to me... listen to me... I can tell you something - that if you do it now, you get rid of the problem! Also, I have dictated six pages with the teacher.
316. T: All at once.
317. S: Eh, just all at once... Cristina told me that so I could get rid of the problem... that's true, otherwise one day you get tired of doing it, in one day, in another half day, and after another half day for only one page... After it is a mess... after you can finish it...

Silvia supports the teacher's requests (line 310) with good arguments, sensitive to the affective burden required by any school work (lines 315, 317). Actually Silvia seems to have also mastered the text composition technique very well, because she is aware that rereading the whole text is essential for going on (line 366 in Text 9).

Text 9

361. T: Now it is enough... Is there someone who wants to continue?
362. S: Yes, I want to.
363. T: Then, Silvia, have you got an idea?
364. S: Will you read it for me?
365. T: So...

366.   S: Will you read it for me? Read it, please, otherwise I
             won't know how to continue...

It can be noted that Silvia (S in Text 5, quoted earlier) made a
tutoring intervention (lines 386, 388) that is more effective than the
nonspecific request for expansion produced by the teacher. She
gives two alternatives for going on with the story ("if you had a good
time or if you didn't have a good time") and succeeds in getting
Giorgio (Gi) going on.

Something similar happened with Gaia (Ga in Text 3 quoted
earlier), who explains the implications (line 73) of the undeveloped
exposition of Katia (line 72) and in so doing coconstructs the story
with her.

Another example of a type of social interaction occurs during
collective text composition, when it is possible to observe an alter-
nation of phases of opposition and coconstruction. The group interaction begins with children debating about the choice between two
verb tenses (imperfect or perfect). They hear the differences, but
they can't give the reasons for them, and the problem remains un-
solved. In the following section, Francesca (the youngest child in
the group) disagrees with Claudio's interpretation by making an observation (line 236) that disconfirms Claudio's interpretation (line
232).

Text 10

228.   Gi: Both arrive and are afraid because something has disap-
             peared...
229.   T: Indeed? Is something missing in this home?
230.   Gi: I don't know.
231.   :   No! (unidentified voice with a prolonged intonation)
232.   C: Yes, the bathroom.
233.   T: (Laughing) The bathroom?
234.   F: Of course not the bathroom! The bathroom is here!
235.   T: She says that there is a bathroom.
236.   F: Look at it! There is a towel in the picture!
237.   Gi: Then what is missing is... is...

The text composition goes on (see Text 11) with another proposal now advanced by Giorgio (line 240), which receives the strong opposition of Silvia (line 244), who considers it ungrounded. At the end of this sequence, Giorgio (line 256) has to build on Gaia's (line 249) proposal, and they both contribute to the story's development.

Text 11

240. Gi: But perhaps handkerchiefs are missing...
241. T: Then handkerchiefs are missing... Hey, Giorgio, do we write down that handkerchiefs are missing?
242. F: Yes.
243. T: Now we write it down... Francesca, in the meanwhile you can put on the paste for the pictures... What will we write?
244. S: No, I do not agree that there are handkerchiefs in a bathroom, because in my bathroom...
245. Gi: I said that handkerchiefs had *disappeared*.
246. F: Ahem, they had disappeared.
247. S: In my bathroom there are no handkerchiefs.
248. C: Not even in mine.
249. Ga: You should say the toilet paper in the bathroom!
250. T: But what has disappeared? Please, toilet paper or handkerchiefs?
251. All: The toilet paper!
252. Gi: Please, the handkerchiefs, because they were not in the bathroom, they were in the pocket of the lady... and she has put them somewhere, and lost them, then...
253. Ga: No, for me toilet paper is much better!
254. Gi: Noo! (with prolonged intonation)
255. T: Toilet paper is more logical but handkerchiefs can be found in a bathroom... please.
256. Gi: Then both... let us do it, let us write both...

Writing construction and interpretation. We will now conclude this exposition with a few examples of peer interaction drawn from writing construction and interpretation that show different examples of *tutoring* that children do with each other. In Text 12, Alessandra (A), who is presyllabic, is helped by Cristina (Cr), who is syllabic but knows how to write certain names alphabetically.

Text 12

354.　　A: */sole/(NOIACIOIOVMONOIA)* (/sun/)

355.　　T: */sole/ Per scrivere... /sole/ tutto questo?* (/sun/ To write... /sun/ all that?)

356.　　Cr: *Ma sei stupido, Alessandra! Guarda! (SOLE)* (But you are stupid, Alessandra! Look at it!)

357.　　A: *Eh... no, voglio scrivere cosi'!* (Eh... no, I want to write it this way!)

358.　　Cr: *Guarda Alessandra te lo scrivo io (prende il suo foglio) ... guarda allora... SOLE* (Look, Alessandra, I will write it for you (he takes his sheet) ... look here... SOLE).

359.　　A: *Ah, allora così (SOLE)?... (inizia a ricopiare) ...la /esse/ S* (Ah, so it is this way...) (he begins copying) ...the /es/ S)

360.　　Cr: *Eh, bravo!* (That's good!)

361.　　A: *la/o/...* O I

362.　　Cr: *No!*

363.　　A: *Mannaggia!* (Damn!)

364.　　Cr: *Va bè, non fa niente... fallo sotto...* (Well, it does not matter... you will do it again under...)

365.　　A: *Sotto? Qui?* (Under? Here?)

366.　　Cr: *Si'.* (Yes.)

367.　　A: C

368.　　Cr: *No, così Alessandra! Così! un' altra lettera... guarda Alessandra... sotto qua...* (No, in this way Alessandra! This is another letter... look Alessandra... under, here...)

369.　　A: *La devo scancellà.* (I have to erase it.)

370.　　T: *Ecco quando una lettera non va bene si cancella no? Non è un problema.* (Then, when a letter does not look good, it can be erased, right? It is not a problem.)

371.　　Fa: *Ma com si cancella?* (But how can it be erased?)

372.   T: *Si fa un taglietto così ...* (You put a line on it.)

373.   A: */Aless.../ .... /sole/ (SOLE)* (He utters part of his name, before writing correctly /<u>SUN</u>/.)

374.   Cr: *Così!* (That's right!)

In another group Gaia (Ga) effectively tutors Maurizio (M), who doesn't know where to begin to read his name (Text 13a). Since Gaia is syllabic, she doesn't succeed in helping Maurizio, who finds problems in reading his name. She writes it down as AUIZIO, and he can't accept it (Text 13b). However with *her* name (which she writes and reads alphabetically), she eventually models the right reading to Maurizio (Text 13c).

Text 13a

127.   Ga: *Guarda... leggimi il tuo nome adesso...* (Look... read your name now.)

128.   M: *Io? Io racconto il tuo nome?* (Me? I have to tell your name?)

129.   Ga: *No, devi leggere il tuo nome... leggilo...* (No, you have to read your name... read it.)

130.   M: *Comincia da qua (O)?* (Does it begin from here (O)?)

131.   Ga: *No, da qua (M).* (No, from here (M).)

132.   M: */ma/ (M)*

133.   F: */u/*

134.   M: */u/ (A) /ri/ (U)...* no, */ma/ (M) /u/ (A) /ri/ (U)...*

135.   Ga: *No... no... ecco non hai contato questa (A).* (No, no, you have not said this one (A).)

136.   M: *Perchè questa (A) non è la /u/!* (Why isn't this (A) the one /u/?)

137.   Ga: *Perchè non lá hai fatta scusa! Non lá hai fatta!* (Because you have not done it! You have not done it!)

Text 13b

283.   Ga: AUIZIO

284.   M: *Incomincia /ma/ ... /ma/ ...* (It begins /ma/ ... /ma/.)

285.   T: */ma/... /ma/...*

286.   Ga: */ma/ (A) /u/ (U) /ri/ (I) /zi/ (Z) /o/ (O)*

287.   T: *Senti, lei lo ha scritto così (AUZIO) è così che si scrive il*

tuo nome? (Listen, she has written it this way (AUZIO).
Is this the way your name is written?)

288. Ga: */ma/ (A) /u/ (U) /i/ (I) /zi/ (Z) /o/ (O)*
289. M: */ma/ (A) /u/ (U) /ri/ (I) /zi/ (Z) /o/ (O)*
290. F: */rizio/ ... /io/ ... Maurizio!*
291. M: *No, non é cosí!* (No, it's not this way!)
292. T: *E' così o no?* (Is is this way or not?)
293. M: *Noo!*
294. T: */Maurizio/... Mi sa che lui veramente lo sa scrivere il
        suo nome, questo è il discorso, che lo sa scrivere... ma
        non lo sa leggere quello è il problema!* (I think that he
        really knows how to write his name. This is the ques-
        tion... he knows how to write it... but he can't read it...
        this is the problem!)

Text 13c

373. M: GAO
374. Ga: *E che cè scritto?* (And what is written here?)
375. M: */gaia/* (He says the name quietly.)
376. Ga: *Come così (GAO) (ironica)? Come così (GAO) lo hai
        scritto te? ... Questa (G) è gíusta.* (What's that (ironi-
        cally)? How have you written it? This (G) is right.)
377. T: *Quella (G) è gíusta.* (This (G) is right.)
378. T: *E questa (G) come si legge? Questa sola letterina (G)?*
        (And how would you read this (G)? This letter alone?)
379. M: */ga/*
380. Ga: */g/*
381. T: */g/ si legge no? ... o si legge /ga/? ... /g/ oppure /ga/?*
        (You read it /g/ or ... /ga/?)
382. F: */gaia/*
383. Ga: */ga/ ... la /ga/ ... /ga/ (G) /a/ (A) /i/ (I) /a/ (A) ...
        /gaia/*

The next example concerns a situation in which there is (subsequent) reciprocal teaching between two children on the writing of
their own names. In Text 14, it is first Claudio (C) who helps Roberto (R) (who is at a beginning syllabic level), and afterwards it is
Roberto who helps Claudio.

Text 14

87. T: *Eh! Di un po' come si chiama... /cla/u/dio/.* (Eh! Say his name... /cla/u/dio/.)
88. R: */ooooooo/... la /o/ O...* (CLUDO)
89. C: *Si, ma ha sbagliato una parola.* (Yes, but he has made a mistake on a word.)
90. T: *Aspetta... aspetta* (Wait... wait.)
91. R: *Dai, quale ho sbagliato?* (Go on, what mistake did I make?)
92. C: *Prima la /a/ ... prima, no..., no... controlla un po' sul mio... sul mio foglio che cè scritto che non hai fatto... hai fatto prima la /u/!* (First the /a/ ... first, no..., no... check my sheet, there is written what you have not done... you have done the /u/ first!)
93. R: (He picks up the sheet of Claudio.) *Ahhh!!*
94. C: *La /a/ ci mancava* (The /a/ was lacking.)
95. T: *Ah, hai capito! ... Perchè? ... per scrivere /cla/ che ci devi mettere?* (Ah, have you understood it? Why? To write it down /cla/ what do you have to put there?)
96. R: */a/ A*
142. R: */b/ ... /e/ ...*
143. T: */di/?*
144. R: (He dictates to Claudio.) */e/... /bu/ e /e/... /bu/ ecco questa!* (Here, this one (B)!)
145. K: *La /e/ e così (E).* (The /e/ goes this way (E).)
146. R: *Guarda come se fa, quarda...* (Look how it has to be done.)
147. C: *Sì, lo so.* (Yes, I know.)
148. K: *La /e/ così (E)!* (The /e/ goes this way (E)!)
149. T: *Finisci Roberto scusa* (Finish it, Roberto, please.)
150. R: *Dai! ... e poi /e/ ... /e/ ... /erre/* (Go on! ... and after /e/ ... /e/ ... /ar/.)
155. C: *Che ci va dopo la /e/?* (What goes after the /e/?)
156. T: *Leggilo quello che hai scritto! Leggi un po'!* (Read now what you have written! Read it now!)
157. C: */r/o/b/e/* (ROBE)
158. R: */erre/* (Ar)

159.   C: /erre/ ... _R_

The last example is an interaction between Gaia (Ga) and Giulio (G), who have to write "gatta" (feminine for cat), after having written their names and "gatto" (masculine for cat). Both have to use the same first letter of their own names, but Giulio has a further problem since his first letter has a different sound (It is not a /g/ but a /dz/). The two children have different strategies. Gaia, who is nearer to the alphabetic system, looks for every single letter without relying on the similarities to her name, while Giulio, although less advanced, draws his information from the word "gatto" that they have already written.

Text 15

474.   T: *Benissimo... allora dobbiamo scrivere /gatta/ adesso.* (Very well... now we have to write /female cat/.)

475.   Ga: E ci vuole... ci vuole /g/ /a/. (And we need... we need /g/ /a/.)

476.   G: /i/... /to/

477.   Ga: /t/ ... /a/ ... /ga/ ... /t/ ... /a/.

478.   T: *E allora scrivilo.* (Then write it down.)

479.   Ga: /g/ ... /g/ ... /g/ ... /g/ ... *qualè la* /g/? (Which is the /g/?)

480.   T: /gatta/ ... *come qualè la* /g/? (Why do you ask which is the /g/?)

481.   G: *È questa (G) no!* (It is this (G), isn't it?)

482.   Ga: *Questa (G)?* (This one (G)?)

483.   T: *E certo... è del tuo nome e abbiamo visto che é uguale a quella di Giulio... Allora...* (It is true, it is from your name and we see that it is similar to that of Giulio. Then...)

484.   Ga: /g/ _G_ /a/ ...

485.   T: /gat/ta/ ... *tu hai scritto* /gatto/ *eh... Giulio controlla un po'* ... (You have already written /male cat/ eh... Giulio, check it...)

486.   Ga: /g/ (G) /a/ _A_... /t/ ... /t/...

487.   T: /gatta/

488.   Ga: /g/a/t/t/t/... /t/...

489.   T: /ga/
490.   Ga: /t/... /t/... /t/... *qualè la /t/?* Which is the /t/?)
491.   G: *Devo fà uguale a questa (GATO)?* (I have to do it the same as this (GATO)?)
492.   Ga: /t/... /t/... /t/... *qualè la /t/?* (Which is the /t/?)
493.   T: *Guarda Giulio... guarda Giulio* (Look at Giulio... look at Giulio.)

Some General Considerations

We have shown how the social context can foster the development of literacy in children and how they can learn to read and write through social interaction with teachers and peers, learning to interact productively with others and to cooperate autonomously, through the different types of social interaction that we call tutoring, coconstructing, and arguing.

We learned from our initial data, drawn from single children and small group observation, that the cognitive level of the child's activity becomes more and more complex. It becomes more planned, monitored, and continuous, ending in some resolution. The complexity increases significantly for all the children in the experimental group as compared with the control group.

It is especially notable that the young children, who entered the program at 4 years of age and who followed during the second year the curriculum described in this chapter, were those who increased more than the other children in their complex cognitive level. In addition, in the group of younger children, a higher level of small group work was independently assessed. Thus, the cognitive development level (as measured by single child observation) can be attributed partly to social interaction effects.

From the observations and interviews collected a year later, the original 4-year-old group's social and conversational skills were especially developed and were expressed by arguing over written language problems and generally by managing autonomous social interactions among themselves, aimed at literacy learning and text production.

We need follow-up results to be able to say that it is better to become literate through this socially explicit process than through a more implicit and individual one. It is certain, however, that children enjoyed their learning and were highly motivated in this social context.

From Psychological Theory to Educational Practice: A Two-Way Relationship

The relationship between psychological theory and educational practice always has been a difficult one. We hope that our work provides some information about psychological processes—both in their individual and social features—that can be implemented during literacy development. Thus, although psychological theory can have a leading role in planning and implementing educational practice, the latter can provide information to the theory, because it offers an ecological setting (Bronfenbrenner, 1979) in which psychological processes are growing and developing.

In other words, we have stressed the role of social interactions in developing the literacy competence of children, but we also think that the social context we described, which can be created in many educational settings, can offer situations in which development can be observed and interpreted.

It is time to look at school settings not only in terms of *outcomes* but also in terms of *processes*. The classroom is a social setting in which it is possible to understand processes of individual cognitive growth that can be affected by social exchanges and supports and by cultural transmission.

From this point of view, educational practice is not only an end point of a theory developed elsewhere but a powerful potential for a psychological theory that takes into account all the environmental variables of development.

(The research described in this chapter is part of an Italian national project directed by Clotilde Pontecorvo and supported by an MPI 40% grant from 1983-1987.)

Applying Psychogenesis Principles
to the Literacy Instruction
of Lower-Class Children in Brazil

T he failure of lower-class students to become literate in Brazil is of primary educational concern. The reasons for the failure include malnutrition, the limitations of a linguistic code, lack of social affection, and possible differences in the logical development between lower-class children and middle- and upper-class children. Since 1979, A Study Group in Education — Methodology, Research, and Action (GEEMPA), has been devoted to investigating literacy among lower-class Brazilian children.

We discovered in our study of young children in the village of Porto Alegre that lower-class children are generally perceived as unable to cope appropriately with the school's requirements. When compared to middle- and upper-class peers, these children have significantly less knowledge about reading and writing. Experience with literacy in their homes is much more limited. Yet, our work shows that these children are quite capable of becoming literate.

The work of Ferreiro and Teberosky (1979) has helped us to understand this problem more comprehensively. Ferreiro and Teberosky note that children begin the process of becoming literate long before they encounter schools and teachers. Children who do not have experiences with books and written materials at home prior to schooling are often at the very beginning of the process of becoming literate when they reach school age. These children will be presyllabic, whereas the children with more experience with print will tend to already be alphabetic in their knowledge about written language.

The children in the GEEMPA project from Porto Alegre have given us further insight into early literacy before schooling and the necessity of changing the often inappropriate didactic process of teaching these lower-class children in school.

The GEEMPA Project

During the past seven years, GEEMPA has been working to expand and develop greater understanding of more appropriate schooling for the pupils in the peripheral areas of Porto Alegre.

The main idea of the GEEMPA literacy program is to give lower-class children, from the first day of school, the opportunity to be involved with a variety of writing and reading materials similar to those found in the homes of middle- and upper-class children before those children enter school.

The GEEMPA program supports the learning processes of the lower-class children and offers them a rich environment of experiences with reading and writing so that each child has the opportunity to reflectively construct his or her writing system. From the very beginning, GEEMPA focuses the learning of literacy on integrating letters and words with texts.

Activities with Texts

Story reading is an essential contact with written texts. Stories are a way of creating a mental image, whereas drawings represent the images on paper. From a drawing, it is possible to construct a story. The process is a complete cycle, shown as follows.

⟳Adult's storytelling > mental image > drawing > writing ⟲

There is an interaction established among drawing, mental images, writing, and speech that promotes a dynamic bond between the oral language and the written text. This condition is necessary to develop the relationships between reading and writing.

Classroom activities are planned with the cycle in mind. The teacher will read a story with or without illustrations and encourage drawing after the reading. Then the teacher and children may write a collaborative summary of the story. The children and teacher in an experimental class write the text together and make drawings and cards together after the reading of the story. An example of one text the children and teacher wrote together follows.

João E Maria

Um dia João e Maria foram para floresta cortar lenha como pai e a maẽ.

A noite João e Maria se perderam.

Ai eles começaram a chorar e encontraram uma casa no meio da floresta. A casa era toda de doces, chocolate e biscoitos.

A bruxa, que morava na casa, ouviu um barulho e perguntou: Quem é que está comendo a minha casinha?

A bruxa abeiu a porta e convidou os dois para entrar. Prendeu o João numa Juala e botou a Maria a fazer o serviço da casa.

Quando ela achou que João estava gordinho, preparou o caldeiraõ. E na hora de colocar Joaõ na panela Maria colocou o pé na frente da bruxa, ela caiu e os dois deram no pé.

Correram...correram e encon—tearam o pai e a mãe na floresta.

E dai voltaram para casa.

Translation
John and Mary

One day, John and Mary went to the woods to cut wood with Daddy and Mommy.

At night, John and Mary got lost.

They started crying; they found a house back in the woods. The house was made of chocolate, candies, and cookies.

A witch that lived in the house heard some noise and asked: "Who is eating in my kitchen?"

The witch opened the door and invited John and Mary to come in. She put John in a cage and forced Mary to clean the house.

When she thought John was fat enough she prepared the big pan, but when she was going to put John in the pan Mary made the witch fall down so they could escape.

They ran and ran. They finally found Daddy and Mommy and went back to the house.

The cards are organized based on the text. They are used with children at different levels as is indicated in the diagram that shows the cycle.

The children tell or write stories with their own drawings. Then they participate in favorite activities with written texts, such as writing favorite songs, sending postcards to others, or receiving postcards from friends and teachers.

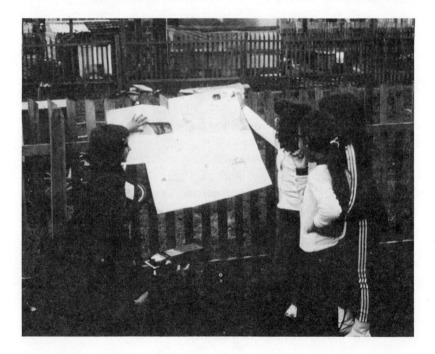

Activities with Words and Letters

Although the major focus is on working with whole texts, instructional episodes that include the writing of isolated words from the text give the child the opportunity to make connections between segments of the oral language and segments of the writing. These activities provide opportunities and experiences with the reading of text so the children can observe the syllabic analysis necessary for their understanding of the written system. As the students focus on words, they begin to make the connections that lead to writing.

Object of speech > mental image > drawing > writing >

As shown by the research of Ferreiro and Teberosky (1982), there are two ways for the figurative form to be present in writing: directly by the graphic representation and indirectly by the association of the number, size, or quality of letters to the characteristics of the forms of the represented object.

When the children do not connect speech and writing, figurative forms are not yet represented. Rather, they use criteria related to the qualities of what is represented through letters to the words. For instance, a girl named Lize said, "My name has 4 letters because I'm very young. My mommy's name must have 10 letters and my daddy's 15 because he is even older than Mommy." Another example is of a boy who was asked how many letters were needed to write the word *bread*. He said, "It depends on the size of it. Bread standing for a loaf of bread is written with more letters than bread standing for rolls."

Therefore, written words are not connected to oral language for children like Lize who are presyllabic. Our main teaching objective, then, is to help the presyllabic children to understand the differences between the figurative graphics of drawing and the symbolic graphics of writing.

To memorize the spelling of a word is of little value compared to understanding how letters are joined in an utterance. Some presyllabic pupils who are able to recognize and spell several words set aside conventional writing when they become syllabic. They then place a letter for each syllable, denying their previous knowledge.

The words we use for instruction and the words from the texts written by the children and the teacher are those most important to the life of the child, such as the teacher's name and the names of all the children in the class. These are powerful teaching aids, especially if the relationship between the children and the teacher is warm and friendly.

The children in the GEEMPA experimental classes learn to recognize the names of their teacher, their school mates, and characters in their stories. When the presyllabic children began in our experimental program, some of them were able to write their names conventionally: ESTHER MIUDINHO DINOMIR GUSTAVO.

Once they began connecting writing and pronunciation, their name writing changed: ET for ESTHER; MUIO, IOIU, or IUIU for MIUDINHO; DNM or IOI for DINOMIR; and GTU for GUSTAVO. The differences between their own syllabic writing and their consistent ability to read the conventional writing of their names turns out to be a rich conflict for these children that leads to new learnings.

Applying Psychogenesis Principles

The children also are involved in activities with letters of the alphabet that are made of different forms and sizes. The letters are made of different materials such as sandpaper, wood, plastic, and cardboard. As children handle the letters, write their names, and play with letter forms, they become familiar with all kinds of words and letters. Finally, activities that highlight individual letters are intended to connect the sounds to the letters so that the children can consider them independent of words or sentences. Both printed and handwritten letters are used because having children move from the use of one type to another facilitates the learning process.

Games are played with written material whenever possible in this rich classroom environment. Badges and name tags are available and are used for many class activities. All classes and all pupils keep a *treasure set of words* significant to their daily lives. These words are selected by the children and are used in many ways. Dictionaries are made by using drawings of objects or words for each letter of the alphabet. Words are used to label items in the environment for functional purposes.

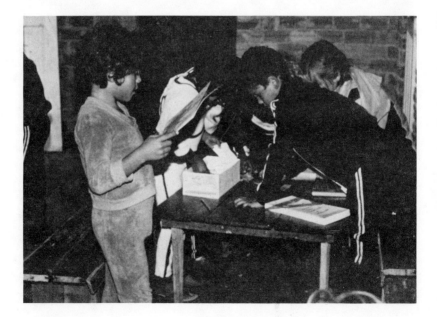

This material and these activities are used throughout the day, and teachers adjust the activities according to what the children know about written representation of language at particular points in time.

Evaluating the Development of Each Child

As we worked with teachers and children in these settings, we noticed some differences between what our children were doing and the results from Ferreiro and Teberosky's studies (1979). We adapted some of their tasks for the GEEMPA project and used them to help teachers organize classroom activities, taking into consideration the development of each child.

The use of these tasks has a different aim from that of the psychogenetic studies. The data provide the teacher with information about each child's knowledge of reading and writing. The teacher tries to connect words to significant experiences in the life of each child. These words are identified after an informal conversation with each child to explore his or her interests during play and leisure time at home. After the words are identified by the teacher, the child is asked to write them. The children usually respond by saying they do not know how to write, but they can draw.

Teacher: Write the word *doll.*
Child: I don't know how to write.
Teacher: Everybody knows how to write a little. Write the way you think it is.
Child: I'd rather make a drawing.

In one of the classes, one child said to another, "Drawing is very important in the first grade because we start writing through drawing."

Over a period of time, we organized levels for our results that differ from those of Ferreiro and Teberosky (1979).

Two Steps of the Presyllabic Level

For the children we worked with, we found it helpful to think of two types of mental organization in the presyllabic levels. In the

Figure 1
Sample of Children's Drawings

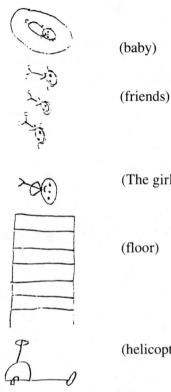

(baby)

(friends)

(The girl is playing house.)

(floor)

(helicopter)

first type, the child understands only the reading of drawings or drawings with letters next to them. The children see both the figurative aspects and the graphic expression as essential to the writing system.

A child who finally realizes that writing is possible only with letters is considered to be in the second stage of the presyllabic level. This child now understands that a graphic sign standing alone can represent something in an abstract way.

We label the two presyllabic levels PS1 and PS2 to categorize the 12 percent of the children in our classrooms who do not distinguish between writing and drawing when they enter school.

Intermediary and Principle Levels

Besides dividing the presyllabic level into two categories, we subdivided some of the other levels described by Ferreiro and Teberosky. There is an intermediary step 1 between presyllabic 1 and presyllabic 2, an intermediary step 2 between presyllabic 2 and the syllabic level, and an intermediary step 3 between the syllabic and the alphabetic levels. During the intermediary steps, the children are conscious as they write that they are now unable to solve a problem that at one time they were able to work out. These difficulties must be overcome during the development of literacy, yet they are important to the learning process. Claparede has pointed out that "conscience springs up from problems" (Jalley, 1981).

A main problem for a presyllabic 1 child is to connect the substitution of written words for drawings. He or she makes a drawing of a particular person — anything or anybody whose written representation is a proper noun and substitutes this for the written form.

As mentioned by Ferreiro and Teberosky (1979), the written names of the child or of other people represent a way to substitute for a drawing with a set of letters. When children generalize this notion, however, they may still think that any graphic sign or set of letters represents any word. At this point in their thinking, the children may focus their attention on the role that the stability of letters plays in written language. They construct hypotheses concerning this issue and, if in a favorable learning setting, may write the conventional form of a number of words. (A favorable setting here is described as one in which the learning material is available for the children to think about and construct hypotheses for.)

At this point, the children are able to represent a whole sequence of letters but do not yet understand how these letters relate to the syllabic structure of the oral form. As they participate in the conventional writing of some words, they often are conscious of uniqueness and stability in word writing. However, the children may be puzzled about the uniqueness and stability in words they do not know well.

This basic conflict will lead children to the syllabic hypothesis as they solve such a problem by representing each segment of the oral word with a letter. In this way, writing any word is temporarily possible. There will be a new conflict when the children become conscious that they can write any word but that it is not always possible to read it. It also seems impossible to read conventional writing because there are too many letters. This problem forces children to begin to consider the nature of the alphabetic writing system. It is through the nature of the children's conflicts that they move toward literacy. These personal conflicts are enhanced by social interactions with the people participating in the literacy events as well as with the objects of literacy.

The Role of Social Interaction

The influences that make possible the passage from one level to another spring from a social awareness that other people understand what is written. When children draw imperfect pictures of themselves or of other people, the drawings are clear to them because they know the person the drawing represents. The fact that other people do not recognize the subject causes the conflict of the passage from the PS1 level to PS2 level.

The same thing occurs when a child in the PS2 level writes words that are not readable by other people. This leads the child to establish social criteria for writing, using the knowledge already constructed that words in the oral language are composed of phonetic segments (oral syllables). These criteria establish a quantitative relationship, associating the pronunciation of each oral syllable with a written letter.

The next conflict is influenced by a social factor and results in the passage from the syllabic level to the alphabetic one. The children understand the meaning of the set of letters that they have generated but realize that it cannot be read by others. This causes them to conclude that the construction of the social object-system of the written language is possible only when there is a social interaction between reading and writing. This interaction becomes essential for the children in the GEEMPA project. Since there are few interactions dealing with writing at home, it is necessary for the teacher to work intensively in the classroom with reading and writing to stimulate social interaction among the children and between the teacher and the children.

Teaching and Cognitive Psychology

One of the specific research tasks of GEEMPA in developing an alternative literacy program is to solve the problem of school failure among lower-class children in Brazil. A new learning approach should establish a correspondence between the discoveries in the field of cognitive psychology regarding literacy and the performance of the teacher in the classroom. All teachers need to have a thoughtful and informed foundation for their actions, even though they may not be able to express them. That is what Freire (1986) means when he says that any educational attitude is a theory of knowledge put into action.

The studies presented in this volume, which are based on Piaget's constructivism, constitute a new theory of knowledge to be put into action in the classroom. A change in cognitive models implies a change in the way these models are used. Based on these new ideas about literacy, how can a new form of teaching be activated?

The GEEMPA project has included as a part of its research design the opportunity for a number of knowledgeable teachers to apply to the classroom setting the most important teaching principles that emerge from the study of literacy development. It is through the actions of these knowledgeable teachers that we have understood more about the presyllabic, syllabic, and alphabetic levels of literacy.

The teaching procedures for each level consist of being aware of what characterizes the thoughts of a child at a particular point in time. These procedures also consist of the teacher's careful questioning strategies that promote the necessary conflict to influence a child's passage to the next level without forcing the child to view literacy learning through the eyes of the adult. By involving the children in literacy opportunities, the teachers are able to identify the

characteristics of the classroom setting that promote not only the construction of hypotheses by the children but also the conflicts that will lead to new hypotheses.

In the five years that GEEMPA has been in operation, we have observed a positive link between the development of children's literacy and informed teaching in a rich literacy environment supported by many reading and writing materials.

The planning of teaching procedures is not the same for every child. Plans take into consideration that the children are at different levels in the process of learning. Using the understanding teachers have of the children as well as of the literacy tasks, it is possible to observe the progress in the children's reading and writing development.

The table that follows shows the development of children in one of the GEEMPA projects at four regular intervals during one year of the study.

In the first evaluation, at the beginning of the school year, none of the children were alphabetic (A), and the majority (28) were not yet syllabic. By the time of the final evaluation, all of the children were at least syllabic (S), and 27 of them were alphabetic.

Table 1
Development of Children in a GEEMPA Project

	PS I	I2	PS2	I2	S	I3	A	TOTAL
First evaluation	2	3	10	13	1	1	0	30
Second evaluation	0	0	8	2	13	2	5	30
Third evaluation	0	0	1	2	2	3	22	30
Final evaluation	0	0	0	0	3	0	27	30

The illustrations that conclude this article show the progression of children developing literacy. It is obvious that the children are at different levels in the same classroom during the school year, but what is most important is that the progress of all of them is obvious. They **all** are capable of becoming literate.

Figure 2
Children's Illustrations
Show Progress toward Literacy

(sun)

ma R O ulo
(9 y 1m)

(car)

televisão
(TV set)

Eu brinco de esconde-esconde meus primos.

(I play hide and seek with my cousin.)

Yetta M. Goodman

Children's Knowledge about Literacy Development: An Afterword

I n the past 20 years, researchers and scholars working in early literacy have constructed a powerful knowledge base, concluding that children come to know literacy through their daily and mundane experiences in their particular social, cultural, religious, economic, linguistic, and literate societies. This conclusion must be recognized as one that should have profound impact on education everywhere in the world.

The psychogenetic work done by Ferreiro and her colleagues has added significantly to the understandings concerning children's active and personal involvement in the development of their own literacy. Other researchers, who come from other theoretical and research traditions, as I summarized in the first chapter, continue to add to the knowledge explosion taking place in the field of literacy development. Authors, publishers, and editors of instructional materials for children, curriculum developers, test producers, researchers in literacy development, and teachers *must* begin to reflect in their work the important lessons that have been learned from the explosion of knowledge about literacy development.

There is general agreement concerning the major concepts that young children are developing about written language, especially among those of us who have been involved in qualitative research. I will summarize some of those concepts and suggest what implications they have for the literacy development of young children and for curriculum development within the school setting. This will lead to some considerations for further research.

Children's Knowledge and the Classroom Environment

All children have some knowledge about literacy as a cultural form, and they have attitudes and beliefs about literacy as a result of their developing concepts about literacy. They know the functions that written language serves, and they know who may participate in its use. Children know what reading is and in what kinds of materials reading can occur. They know who reads, where people read, what different people use reading for, and who can and cannot read. Children know what writing is and what kinds of forms writing takes. They know who writes, what people write with, and what people use writing for.

I use the term *know* to refer to the tacit knowledge children have about language rather than their explicit knowledge. Human action is strongly influenced by intuitive or tacit knowledge—the understandings people have about their universe but are unable to discuss with others. Children are able to discuss certain aspects of their knowledge and ideas about reading and writing with others, but they are unable to put into words most of what they know about written language. Children come to know language within the context of their own culture, society, family, and socioeconomic group, which strongly influences their views and beliefs about who is literate and who may become literate.

Children also come to know that reading and writing in school is often different from reading and writing outside of school. They sometimes, unfortunately, come to believe that the instructional reading and writing activities inside of school are "real reading and writing" and that the actual literacy events that occur daily in their own lives are somehow of lesser status.

It is of utmost importance that the people involved in organizing school experiences for young children take into consideration what the children know about literacy. Too many kindergarten and first grade classrooms still are organized as if children come to school without any knowledge of literacy (Durkin, 1987; Heath,

1983). Basal readers, workbooks, and reading readiness activities for the very young ignore the experiences children have with reading and writing before school and treat all children as empty slates (Goodman et al., 1988).

Classrooms need to reflect the rich literate environments in which children are immersed outside of school. There need to be signs that label materials for children to use; labels for areas where children store their belongings; books and magazines to read; and various sizes, shapes, and colors of paper that children can write on in appropriate ways in their play, their cooking, and their independent time activities.

All learning experiences need to be organized so that they invite children to participate in literacy events as a legitimate and significant part of their daily academic learnings (Loughlin & Martin, 1987). Teachers need to point out to children, as the knowledgeable teacher does in *When Will I Read?* (Cohen, 1977), that they are reading and writing all the time.

> "When will I read?" Jim asks.
> "Soon," the teacher said.
> "But when?" said Jim.
> "You know what the signs in our room say," the teacher said.
> "Yes," said Jim, "I know. 'Please put the blocks back when you are done'
> and 'Don't let the hamsters out' "(pp. 2-3).

Authentic literacy events need to become the focus of the school day as children:

- sign in daily so that the teacher knows who has arrived in school;
- put away their materials in appropriate settings, using the signs in the room or their names on their cubbies;
- read recipes and menus as they cook, eat, and learn about healthy nutritional activities;
- write prescriptions at the play hospital or take phone messages in the house corner; and
- read storybooks, write letters, and record observations.

We have long known in early childhood circles that play is the work of children, but we continue to let those who cry for didactic academic hierarchies divert our attention from what we know best supports children's learning. There is much to play at in literacy learning.

Children play at using literacy events in their wheel toy areas as they write receipts for gasoline put into the rear of the tricycle, in their doll corners as they read to their dolls or play doctor and write prescriptions for sick babies, and in their play stores as they label the shelves or fill orders from shopping lists.

At the same time that children play using reading and writing, they experiment with the forms of reading and writing itself: how to form the letters, where the spaces go, and what purposes conventional spelling and punctuation serve. This kind of playing with written language supports their developing schema about written language.

Children's Knowledge and the Curriculum

Literacy development is as complex, dynamic, and important for the history of the individual as literacy development has been for the history of all of human society. Written language was developed and continues to be developed by human society in response to various social, cultural, economic, and political needs. Written language is invented by children in a literate environment in response to their own social and cultural needs as they interact with the objects of literacy in the society and with the literate members of society.

There are developmental moments in the literacy development of the individual that parallel in complex ways the development of literacy for the human race. Children first begin to understand that writing is a representational system that is different from drawing. Originally, they seem to think of the writing system as logographic; that is, each symbol, as defined by the child, represents some idea or concept that is meaningful and familiar to the child.

Children who live in an alphabetical, literate environment begin to hypothesize that there are relationships between oral and written language. They speculate that there is a relationship between certain aspects of oral segmentation and certain segments of the writing system, using their own categories based on their developing schema about linguistic units. This initially represents a syllabic view of language. Later, the children develop an awareness of the alphabetic nature of language; they learn that there is a complex representation between the sound system of the language and the graphic system. They are concerned with the way something sounds in relation to how it looks. Although what the children come to know about the writing system is influenced by the nature of the writing system in which the child is immersed, there are universal rules that all children seem to conceptualize in similar ways at particular developmental moments in their personal history.

Developmental moments are influenced by sociocultural experiences such as: language variations, both written and oral; functions of literacy in the particular social group and within the society at large; socioeconomic and political issues of the power of literacy; personal experiences; and instructional practices.

Children are actively involved in developing these constructions of written language. Adults, especially teachers in schools, are important influences because they either can support the children's constructions or help children believe that their constructions are not valid.

When educational practitioners seriously take into consideration the ramifications of what they know about how children construct written language, they can support and facilitate literacy development. As concerned teachers and other educational practitioners examine what they know about literacy development, they become more consciously aware of their influences on the learning of their students. They appreciate the strengths children have in controlling their own learning. They observe how children invent their own knowledge about the processes of reading and writing. They take advantage of the many opportunities to collaborate with children in their literacy experiences through talk and other kinds of interactions as they read and write together in the social community of the classroom.

Teachers with knowledge about literacy development know that they do not have to spend a year or more getting children ready to read or write with activities that have little payoff in literacy development. They know that children learn to read and write as they *use* reading and writing to learn. Teachers know that children learn about language and can begin to talk about language as they use language to learn about the world. The classroom becomes a dynamic learning environment, not a waiting room where children are asked to get ready to do something that they really know how to do already.

Knowledgeable teachers do not consider that planning a list of "doing activities" or language games related to amassing knowledge about specific words, letters, or definitions of vocabulary items is tantamount to curriculum development. Rather, such observant teachers organize environments and plan thematic units through which children speak, listen, read, and write in order to think about problems and try to solve them, to answer self-generated questions, and to wonder about the world in areas significant to their daily lives.

Teachers become careful observers of children's interactions with written language and participate in informal kinds of research in their own classrooms. They learn to recognize those aspects of literacy development that have been written about in the field, and they know when they have discovered something that may represent new issues relating to literacy development.

As teachers become more knowledgeable about the nature of both oral and written language learning and child development, they are more able to perceive the moments of development as they occur in the children. Through this awareness, teachers become adept at asking appropriate questions that will help the children reflect on their knowledge and propel them toward disequilibrium and ever-expanding construction about the nature of literacy.

Professional development programs for preservice and inservice teachers need to include opportunities to develop proficiency in questioning strategies similar to those used in the clinical approach of the Piagetians. Teachers' careful questioning can help show children where their contradictions are, move them toward rethinking, and assist reconstruction of their conceptualizations. On the other hand, similar questions that are asked casually, without sensitivity and understanding about the child's knowledge and attitudes about a particular literacy event, can make children feel insecure about their personal constructions.

Teachers need a lot of experiences to develop the understanding to know when to use specific types of questioning strategies. Teachers can experiment with various questioning techniques to discover which are the most useful at particular times and to understand when children are better off left to their own individual explorations or development through collaborations with peers. Research on teacher questioning strategies could provide more information in this important area of interaction between children and teachers.

Further Research Possibilities

Research in the classroom can take on the dynamic nature of a community of learners such as the ones Teberosky, Pontecorvo and Zucchermaglio, and Grossi (this volume) are studying, in which students and teachers collaborate and learn together from interactions, observations, and struggles. Research becomes a continuous adventure as teachers and researchers inquire together about literacy development.

Controversies about how to focus instructional experiences can be resolved in such settings. In her chapter, Teberosky (this volume) raises some issues about the role of instruction and concludes that years of practice help teachers to overcome the temptation of wondering how to get children to the next level.

Teberosky then goes on to suggest that careful selection of the types of materials and messages used with the children helps them focus more or less on different kinds of linguistic features. On the other hand, in the program Grossi describes in her chapter, teachers use the Ferreiro and Teberosky tasks, developed to discover what children know about language, to help focus the children's attention on isolated linguistic units once they have been generated as part of real literacy events. This is done because of the concern that children who come to school with minimal involvement in literacy events in their homes need to become more attuned to the graphic features of written language.

The research community is now at a point where the contradictory issues raised by Teberosky and Grossi can be explored, if not resolved. Interactive classroom research, using clinical approaches in response to the activity of learning itself, will allow researchers to begin to ascertain the necessity of focusing children's attention on decontextualized letters and words at some point during their instruction and decide whether immersion in authentic literacy experiences provides sufficient opportunities for all children to develop the knowledge they need about literacy to become readers and writers.

The examination of learning activities in the classroom as a research methodology needs to be legitimatized. The dynamic nature of social interactions in classroom settings provides more important data and insights about the influence on literacy development of the social community, the materials being used, and the kinds of interaction patterns than can be observed in one-on-one interview situations.

It is unfortunate when research in such social settings is not considered serious, legitimate, and of high quality. With the baseline of data about literacy development now available, and with legitimatized structures to examine activities in classroom settings, we can begin to base conclusions about applications to learning in school on insights that come directly from research in classroom settings within the dynamic context in which learning occurs. The role of teachers, peers of various abilities, types of instructional materials, discourse patterns, and their influence on literacy development all need to be explored in greater depth and over time.

Of course, the search for knowledge about what children know about literacy development must continue. There are many different languages in the world and many different sociocultural climates that must be examined in order to support the universality of the ways in which children come to know literacy or to suggest what influences the different ways children develop literacy.

The authors in this book have raised new questions about literacy development research and its implications for classroom practice. We hope that the conclusions discussed, the interpretations provided, the issues raised, and the questions that have been asked have pushed all of us, readers and authors, toward new disequilibrium. Our responses to our disequilibrium should lead us to new conceptualizations and new adaptations of knowledge, with the beneficiaries being teachers and children in the classroom as well as the state of worldwide literacy.

References Cited in This Book

Anderson, A., & Stokes, S. (1984). Social and institutional influences on the development and practice of literacy. In H. Goelman, A. Oberg, & F. Smith (Eds.), *Awakening to literacy.* Portsmouth, NH: Heinemann.

Bettelheim, B., & Zelan, K. (1982). *On learning to read: The child's fascination with meaning.* New York: Knopf.

Bissex, G. (1980). *Gyns at wrk.* Cambridge, MA: Harvard University Press.

Blachowicz, C.L.Z., & Pontecorvo, C. (1982). Reading education: Report from Italy. *Reading Psychology, 3,* ix.

Blanche-Benveniste, C. (1984). La dénomination dans le Français parlé: Une interprétation pour les "répétitions" et les "hésitations." *Recherches sur le Français parlé, No. 6.* Aix-en-Provence, France.

Blanche-Benveniste, C. (1982). La escritura del lenguaje dominguero. In E. Ferreiro & M. Gómez-Palacio (Eds.), *Nuevas perspectivas sobre los procesos de lectura y escritura.* México: Siglo xxi.

Blanche-Benveniste, C. (1987). Le Français parlé: Transcription et édition. C. Blanche-Benveniste et C. Jeanjean; pref. Jacques Monfrin-Didier-Erudition. Paris: Institut National Langue Française.

Blanche-Benveniste, C., & Jeanjean, C. (1980). *Evaluation comparée des moyens d'éxpression lingüistique d'enfants Francophones et non Francophones d'origine, dans les mêmes classes.* (Recherche No. 14.01.) Paris, France: Ministère d'Education.

Bronfenbrenner, U. (1979). *The ecology of human development.* Cambridge, MA: Harvard University Press.

Bruner, J.S. (1986). *Actual minds, possible words.* Cambridge, MA: Harvard University Press.

Cazden, C.B. (1972). *Child language and education.* Chicago: Holt.

Chafe, W.L. (1979, August). *Integration and involvement in spoken and written language.* Paper presented at the second congress of the International Association for Semiotic Studies, Vienna, Austria.

Childs, C.P., & Greenfield, P.M. (1980). Informal modes of learning and teaching: The case of Zinanteco Weaving. In N. Warren (Ed.), *Studies in cross cultural psychology: Vol. 2.* New York: Academic Press.

Chomsky, C. (1970). Reading and phonology. *Harvard Educational Review, 40,* 287.

Clark, M.M. (1976). *Young fluent readers.* Portsmouth, NH: Heinemann.

Clay, M. (1975). *What did I write?* Portsmouth, NH: Heinemann.

Cohen, M. (1977). *When will I read?* New York: Greenwillow.

Damon, W. (1984). Peer education: The untapped potential. *Journal of Applied Developmental Psychology, 5,* 331-343.

Derrida, J. (1967). *De la grammatologie.* Paris: de Minuit.

Donaldson, M. (1978). *Children's minds.* London: Fontana.

Downing, J. (1971). Children's developing concepts of spoken and written language. *Journal of Reading Behavior, 4,* 1.

Durkin, D. (1987). Testing in kindergarten. *The Reading Teacher, 40,* 766-771.

Dyson, A. (1982). Reading, writing and language: Young children solving the written language puzzle. *Language Arts, 59,* 829.

Dyson, A. (1985). Three emergent writers and the school curriculum: Coping and other myths. *The Elementary School Journal, 85,* 497.

Ehri, L.C. (1975). Word consciousness in readers and prereaders. *Journal of Educational Psychology, 67,* 204-212.

Ehri, L.C. (1976). Word learning in beginning readers and prereaders: Effects of form class and defining contexts. *Journal of Educational Psychology, 68,* 832-842.

Eisenberg, A., & Garvey, C. (1981). Children's use of verbal strategies in resolving conflicts. *Discourse Processes, 4,* 149.

Erickson, F. (1986). Qualitative methods in research on teaching. In M.C. Wittrock (Ed.), *Handbook of research on teaching* (3rd ed.). New York: Macmillan, 119-161.

Fauconnier, G. (1984). Espaces mentaux, aspects de la construction du sens dans les langues naturelles. Paris: eds. de Minuit.

Ferreiro, E. (1986). The interplay between information and assimilation in beginning literacy. In W. Teale & E. Sulzby (Eds.), *Emergent literacy: Writing and reading*. Norwood, NJ: Ablex.

Ferreiro, E. (1985). Literacy development: A psychogenetic perspective. In D.R. Olson, N. Torrance, & A. Hildyard (Eds.), *Literacy, language and learning: The nature and consequences of reading and writing*. Cambridge, MA: Cambridge University Press.

Ferreiro, E. (1982a). *Literacy development: The construction of a new object of knowledge*. Paper presented at the Twenty-Seventh Annual Convention of the International Reading Association, Chicago, IL.

Ferreiro, E. (1982b). Los procesos constructivos de apropiación de la escritura. In E. Ferreiro & M. Gómez Palacio (Eds.), *Nuevas perspectivas sobre los procesos de lectura y escritura*. México: Siglo xxi.

Ferreiro, E. (1984). The underlying logic of literacy development. In H. Goelman, A. Oberg, & F. Smith (Eds.), *Awakening to literacy*. Portsmouth, NH: Heinemann.

Ferreiro, E. (1978). What is written in a written sentence: A developmental answer. *Journal of Education, 160, 4,* 25-34.

Ferreiro, E. (1986). The interplay between information and assimilation in beginning literacy. In W. Teale & E. Sulzby (Eds.), *Emergent literacy: Writing and reading*. Norwood, NJ: Ablex.

Ferreiro, E., & Teberosky, A. (1982). *Literacy before schooling*. Exeter, NH: Heinemann.

Ferreiro, E., & Teberosky, A. (1979). *Los sistemas de escritura en el desarrollo del niño*. México: Siglo xxi.

Freire, P. (1986). *Pedagogía del oprimido* (34th ed.). México: Siglo xxi.

Freeman, Y.S., & Whitsell, L.R. (1985). What preschoolers already know about print. *Educational Horizons, 64,* 1, 22-24.

Gardner, H. (1980). *Artful scribbles*. New York: Basic Books.

GEEMPA. (1988). *Alfabetizaçaño em classes populares*. Porto Alegre: Editora Kuarup.

Genishi, C., & Di Paolo, M. (1982). Learning through argument in a preschool. In L.C. Wilkinson (Ed.), *Communicating in the classroom*. New York: Academic Press 49-68.

Gesell, A., & Ilg, F. (1946). *The child from five to ten*. New York: Harper.

Gibson, E., & Levin, H. (1975). *The psychology of reading*. Cambridge, MA: MIT Press.

Goodman, K., Shannon, P., Freeman, Y., & Murphy, S. (1988). *Report card on basal readers*. Katonah, NY: Richard C. Owen Publishers.

Goodman, Y. (1982). La escritura en niños muy pequeños. In E. Ferreiro & M. Gómez-Palacio (Eds.), *Nuevas perspectivas sobre los precesos de lectura y escritura*. México: Siglo xxi.

Goodman, Y. (1980). The roots of literacy. In M. Douglass (Ed.), *Reading: A humanizing experience*. Claremont, CA: Claremont Reading Conference.

Goodman, Y., & Altwerger, B. (1981). *Print awareness in pre-school children: A working paper* (Occasional paper No. 4). Tucson, AZ: Program in Language and Literacy.

Goodman, Y., Haussler, M., & Strickland, D. (1981). *Oral and written language development research: Impact on the schools*. Proceedings from the 1979 and 1980 IMPACT conferences. Washington, DC: National Institute of Education. (ED 214 184)

Gough, P.B. (1972). One second of reading. In J.F. Kavanagh & I.G. Mattingly (Eds.), *Language by ear and by eye*. Cambridge, MA: MIT Press.

Grieve, R., Tumner, W.E., & Pratt, C. (1983). Language awareness in children. In M. Donaldson, R. Grieve, & C. Pratt (Eds.), *Early childhood development and education*. New York: Basil Blackwell.

Harste, J., Woodward, V., & Burke, C. (1984). *Language stories and literacy lessons*. Portsmouth, NH: Heinemann.

References

Heath, S.B. (1983). *Ways with words.* Cambridge, MA: Cambridge University Press.
Hildreth, G. (1936). Developmental sequence in name writing. *Child Development, 7,* 291-303.
Hjelmslev, L. (1963). Prolegomena to a theory of language. Madison, WI: University of Wisconsin Press.
Iredell, H. (1898). Eleanor learns to read. *Education, 19,* 233.
Jaggar, A., & Smith-Burke, T. (1985). *Observing the language learner.* Newark, DE: International Reading Association.
Jakobson, R., & Halle, M. (1956). *Fundamentals of language.* Mouton, The Hague.
Jalley, W. (1981). *Lecteur de Freud et Piaget.* Paris: Edition Sociales, 395.
Jeanjean, C. (1985). Toi quand tu souris: Analyse sémantique et syntaxique d'une structure du Français pev étudiée. *Recherches sur le Français parlé, No. 6,* 131.
Kamii, C. (1986). *Spelling in kindergarten: A constructivist analysis comparing Spanish and English-speaking children.* Unpublished manuscript.
Kellogg, R. (1969). *Analyzing children's art.* Palo Alto, CA: National Press Books.
Legrun, A. (1932). Wie und was schreiben Kindergartenzöglinge? *Leitschrift für pädagogische Psychologie, 33,* 322.
Lerner de Zunino, D. (1982, November). *Una propuesta didactica centrada en el proceso espontáneo de construcción de la lengua escrita.* Paper presented at I Jornada de Lectura, Caracas, Venezuela.
Levin, I., & Tolchinsky Landsmann, L. (1989). *Literacy in preschoolers: Referential elements in writing and reading.* In press.
Loughlin, C., & Martin, M. (1987). *Supporting literacy.* New York: Teachers College Press.
Ludwig, O. (1983). Writing systems and written language. In F. Coulmas & K. Ehlich (Eds.), *Writing in focus.* New York: Mouton Publishers.
Luria, A.R. (1980). *Higher cortical functions in man.* New York: Basic Books.
Mason, J. (1980). When do children read: An exploration of four year old children's letter and word reading competencies. *Reading Research Quarterly, 15,* 203.
Michaels, S., & Collins, I. (1984). Oral discourse styles: Classroom interaction and the acquisition of literacy. In D. Tannen (Ed.), *Coherence in spoken and written discourse.* Norwood, NJ: Ablex.
Ninio, A. (1980). Ostensive definition in vocabulary teaching. *Child Language, 7,* 565.
Ninio, A., & Bruner, J. (1978). The achievement and antecedents of labelling. *Child Language, 7,* 565.
Ochs, E. (1979). Planned and unplanned discourse. In T. Givon (Ed.), *Discourse and syntax, Vol. 12.* New York: Academic Press.
Olson, D., & Hildyard, A. (1985). Oral and written language development. In D.R. Olson, N. Torrance, & A. Hildyard (Eds.), *Literacy, language and learning: The nature and consequences of reading and writing.* Cambridge, MA: Cambridge University Press.
Perfetti, C. (1984). Reading acquisition and beyond: Decoding includes cognition. *American Journal of Education, 93,* 40.
Pétrucci, A. (1978). Per la storia dell' alfabetismo e della cultura scritta. *Quaderni Storici, 38.*
Piaget, J. (1971). *Biology and knowledge: An essay on the relations between organic regulations and congitive processes.* Chicago: University of Chicago.
Piaget, J. (1977). *The development of thought: Equilibrium of cognitive structures.* New York: Viking.
Piaget, J. (1958). *Etudes d'épistémologie génétique, V.* Paris: Presses Universitaires.
Piaget, J. (1976). *The grasp of consciousness: Action and concept in the young child.* Cambridge, MA: Harvard University Press.
Piaget, J. (1979). La psychogènese des connaissances et sa signification épistémologique. In M. Piatelli-Palmarini (Ed.), *Théories du langage, théories de l'apprentissage.* Paris: Seuil.
Pinnell, G.S., & Matlin, M. L. (Eds.). (1989). *Teachers and research: Language learning in the classroom.* Newark, DE: International Reading Association.

Pontecorvo, C. (1987). Discussing for reasoning: The role of argument in knowledge construction. In E. DeCorte, J.G.L.C. Lodewijks, R. Parmentier, & P. Span (Eds.), *Learning and instruction*. Oxford/Leuven: Pergamon Press/Leuven University Press.

Pontecorvo, C. (1985). Figure, parole, numeri: Un problema di simbolizzazione. *Età Evolutiva*, 22.

Pontecorvo, C. (1986). Interazione di gruppo e conoscenza: Processi e ruoli. *Età Evolutiva*, 24.

Pontecorvo, C., & Zucchermaglio, C. (1986, November). *From oral to written language: A longitudinal study of preschool children dictating a story*. Paper presented at the National Reading Conference, Austin, TX.

Pontecorvo, C., & Zucchermaglio, C. (1988). Modes of differentiation in children's writing construction. *European Journal of Psychology of Education, 3*, 371-384.

Read, C. (1975). Children's categorization of speech sounds in English. (Research Report No. 17). Urbana, IL: National Council of Teachers of English.

Saussure, R. (1916). *Cours de lingüistique générale*. Lausanne et Paris: Payot.

Schieffelin, B., & Cochran-Smith, M. (1984). Learning to read culturally: Literacy before schooling. In H. Goelman, A. Oberg, & F. Smith (Eds.), *Awakening to literacy*. Portsmouth, NH: Heinemann.

Scinto, L. (1986). *Written language and psychological development*. London: Academic Press.

Scollon, S., & Scollon, R. (1984). Run trilogy: Can Tommy read? In H. Goelman, A. Oberg, & F. Smith, *Awakening to literacy*. Portsmouth, NH: Heinemann.

Smith, F. (1977). Making sense of reading and of reading instruction. *Harvard Educational Review, 47*, 386-396.

Smith, F. (1973). *Psycholinguistics and reading*. New York: Holt.

Smith, F. (1971). *Understanding reading*. New York: Holt, Rinehart & Winston.

Tannen, D. (1982). Oral and literate strategies in spoken and written narratives. *Language, 58*, 1.

Taylor, D. (1983). *Family literacy*. Portsmouth, NH: Heinemann.

Taylor, D., & Dorsey-Gaines, C. (1988). *Growing up literate: Learning from inner-city families*. Portsmouth, NH: Heinemann, 1-20.

Teale, W., & Sulzby, E. (1986). *Emergent literacy: Writing and reading*. Norwood, NJ: Ablex.

Thorndike, R. (1974-1975). Reading as reasoning. *Reading Research Quarterly, 9*, 135-147.

Tolchinsky Landsmann, L., & Levin, I. (1982). El desarrollo de la escritura lu niños Israelies prescolares. In E. Ferreiro, M. Gomez, & O. Palaci (Eds.), *Nuevas perspectivas sobre los procesos de lectura y escritura*. México: Siglo xxi.

Tolchinsky Landsmann, L., & Levin, I. (1987). Writing in four to six year olds: Representation of semantic and phonetic similarities and differences. *Journal of Child Language, 14*, 127-144.

Tolchinsky Landsmann, L., & Levin, I. (1985). Writing in preschoolers: An age related analysis. *Applied Psycholinguistics, 6*, 319.

Vachek, J. (1982). English orthography: A functionalist approach. In W. Haas (Ed.), *Standard languages*. Manchester, NY: Manchester University Press.

Vygotsky, L.S. (1974). *Istorija Razvitija Vyssib Psibiceskib Funktcij*. Mosca Accademia delle Scienze Pedagogiche; trad. it. Storia dello Sviluppo delle funzioni psichiche superiori, Firenze, Giunti-Barbera.

Vygotsky, L.S. (1978). *Mind in society* (M. Cole, V. John-Steiner, S. Scribner, & E. Souberman, Eds. and Trans.). Cambridge, MA: Harvard University Press.

Vygotsky, L.S. (1987) *Thought and language* (A. Kozulin, Trans.). Cambridge, MA: MIT Press.

Wells, G. (1986). *The meaning makers*. Portsmouth, NH: Heinemann.

Zucchermaglio, C., & Formisano, M. (1986, September). *Literacy development and social interaction*. Paper presented at the Second European meeting of the International Society for the Study of Behavioral Development, Rome, Italy.

References   127